LOVE AND LISTS

(Chocoholics #1)

Tara Sivec

Elaine—
Just say no
to weird sex!

♡ tara ♥

Edits by The Polished Pen
http://www.polished-pen.com/

Cover Art by Tara Sivec

Interior Design by Angela McLaurin, Fictional Formats
https://www.facebook.com/FictionalFormats

Also by Tara Sivec

Seduction and Snacks (Chocolate Lovers #1)
Futures and Frosting (Chocolate Lovers #2)
Troubles and Treats (Chocolate Lovers #3)
Hearts and Llamas (Chocolate Lovers Short Story)
Chocolate Lovers Special Edition
A Beautiful Lie (Playing With Fire #1)
Because of You (Playing With Fire #2)
Watch Over Me

Table of Contents

For Tyler: thanks for letting me steal your name.
Kick some ass in the Air Force and make sure everyone knows
how cool you are now.

Gavin

Chapter 1

- The List -

Can someone die from a severe case of blue balls?

Yep, that just happened. I just typed that exact phrase into the Google search engine.

My mother always warned me to stay away from Google. She told me it was the devil. I'm twenty-five years old and I still don't listen to my mother.

According to Wiki, the answer is NO. Just, no. Period. The end. No explanation whatsoever. You would think the person answering these questions could have elaborated just a little bit. Like, "No. You cannot die from blue balls, you fucking moron. Why the hell are you even asking this question? You do realize your internet history can and will be seen by everyone you know at some point in your life, right?"

Note to self: delete internet history. I need to consult my

mom on this. I believe I came across a contract between her and my Aunt Liz a few years ago ...

You're probably wondering why I'm curious if someone can die from blue balls. You're probably also wondering how in the hell I can possibly be twenty-five years old when just yesterday I was four. I know, it's a tough pill to swallow. I'm not a foul-mouthed, cute little kid anymore. I'm now a foul-mouthed, cute adult. I take after my parents, so obviously I'm good looking. That might sound conceited to you, but oh well. I'm not one of those guys who are all "Awwwww, shucks. You really think I'm good looking? Naaaaah, I'm just me."

Fuck that.

I walked around for most of my childhood talking about my penis to anyone who would listen. Owning it when people say I'm hot isn't conceited. It's me being comfortable with who I am.

So anyway, where were we? Oh, right. Penis. Blue balls. Death by blue balls. There's only one reason for my earlier Google question: Charlotte Gilmore. The most beautiful woman I've ever met and my best friend. She's the oldest daughter of my parents' best friends, Liz and Jim Gilmore. She has long, dark brown hair, big gorgeous brown eyes, and a body that takes my breath away. Since we're only three years apart in age, we grew up together. I've been told that we used to take baths together when we were little. Obviously the times we were naked in the tub never left a lasting impression on her since no matter how hard I try, I can't get her to see me as anything other than a friend. The kiss of death. The "friend" curse.

It's all her fault that I even have blue balls, although to be honest, I really shouldn't blame her. It's not like she knows she's causing me extreme pain. She has no idea that every time I'm within three feet of her my penis perks up like a meerkat when it hears a noise. It's fucking Meerkat Manor in my pants. My penis is like a magnet and she's a hot piece of steel. As soon as she walks into a room, the magnetic pull begins and I feel like I have to hold on tight to something. Otherwise, my penis will drag my body over to her and slam itself up against her, like a dog grunting and humping some poor, unsuspecting person's leg. I'm like a fucking dog in heat when it comes to her. My poor penis wants to hump her leg and she just wants to be friends. I feel bad for my penis. He's had a rough life. I love my penis and he's totally getting the shaft. Ha! See what I did there?

Anyway, I know what you're thinking. Who doesn't love their penis? But this is serious, yo. My mom still tells me stories about when I was a little boy and how much I talked about my penis. I'm an adult and I have to worry about inviting my mother to public events for fear she'll tell everyone the story about how I got my first boner to Barney the Dinosaur. Do you have any idea how mortifying that is? A fucking purple dinosaur. Why couldn't I be normal and get excited about the Victoria's Secret catalog like all my friends? To this day, when I see a dinosaur, no matter what I'm doing, my penis instantly retracts itself up inside my body in fear. Even my penis is ashamed.

So, anyway, where was I? Oh yeah, my penis. I get it. I'm a guy and guys think about their penises a lot. Maybe I'd feel better about this obsession if I had someone touching it other than myself. I grew up surrounded by girls. All of my friends are girls. Everywhere I look there are girls. And yet, I still go home alone every night and touch my own penis.

Okay, I don't touch it every night. That's overkill. Maybe once a week.

Okay FINE! Every *other* night. I think the problem is my job. I love my job, I really do. It's not something I grew up dreaming about doing, but I'm good at it, and I make a pretty decent living doing it considering I've only been out of college for a few years.

As some of you know, my mom is a pretty famous person. She owns a huge chain of bakeries around the world. She taught me everything I know about cooking and covering things in chocolate. I always knew I would go into the family business when I got older, and I did. No, not that family business. The *other* one. Are you sitting down for this? Maybe you should be sitting down. I, Gavin Ellis, am the Creative Director for one of the largest sex toy stores in the world. I may have forgot to mention that the chain of bakeries my mom owns is connected to a chain of adult toy stores called Seduction and Snacks. Charlotte's mom, Liz, owns that side of the business.

So, while I don't actually work in a store selling dildos, I'm in charge of the entire product development process for every single item Seduction and Snacks sells. Considering the fact that my job has made me a genius when it comes to pleasuring a woman, and I know the inner workings of every single toy ever made, you would think that women would be throwing themselves at me. Yeah, so not the case. You try being in a bar flirting with a chick and see the look on her face when you tell her you touch rubber penises all day. They all think I'm gay. Or a creeper. Like I'm going to just whip a dildo out of my back pocket and chase her around the room with it. That only happened once, and I was really drunk. I swear.

And that's me in a nutshell, since the last time you heard about me. Tonight, I spent three hours with Charlotte and let her cry on my shoulder because she got into a fight with Rocco, her boyfriend.

"So did you guys break up or something?"

Please say yes, please say yes.

Charlotte cried harder and pressed her face into the side of my neck while I wrapped my arms around her and held her close.

Is it wrong that I'm thinking about pushing her back onto the couch and making out with her instead of consoling her? I suck.

"He just doesn't understand me, you know?" Charlotte whimpered and burrowed closer to me.

You're right. He doesn't understand you. I'm the only one who understands you. ME!

"Did you just say *me?*" Charlotte questioned, pulling her face away from my neck and staring up at me.

"Uh, yes. Me totally understand that he doesn't understand you. Me understand."

I patted her back lamely and tried to think of something un-caveman-like to say next.

"What did you guys fight about?"

I couldn't care less but I'm a good guy and good guys ask these sorts of questions.

Charlotte sighed and scooted away from me on the couch, brushing her long brown hair out of her face. "I don't know. I don't even remember. It was something stupid. I shouldn't have come over here and unloaded all of this on you. He really does love me and he's a great guy."

She looked up at me with wide, expectant eyes, waiting for me to agree with her that he's a super human being. Yeah, not gonna happen.

He's a troll who gets to touch her whenever he wants. He can burn in the fiery pits of hell for all I care.

Charlotte kept looking at me with those gorgeous eyes, and I caved under the pressure.

"You're right. He's awesome. I'm sure you guys will be fine."

Someone get me a bucket to barf in.

I'm jealous, irritated, and horny after holding her so close to me all night and smelling her skin. She always smells like cherry almond. And since I'm slightly obsessed with her, I know that's because of the lotion she uses: Jergens Original Scent. No, that's not weird at all. Shut up. It's probably weird, though, that I stroke the snake using Jergens Original Scent. How about we just pretend I never shared that little tidbit, okay?

My best friend, Tyler Branson, called me when I was on my way home from consoling Charlotte, and he could tell by the sound of my voice that I needed help, so he made an emergency trip to my apartment.

"I think what we need to do here is make a list," Tyler tells me after he swallows a mouthful of beer.

Tyler was my college roommate. I met him on my first day when I moved into the dorms. I walked into our room with my mom and dad carrying boxes of my crap behind me, only to find him standing naked in the middle of his bed, hanging a poster of Megan Fox on his ceiling.

Tyler likes being naked. Tyler thinks everyone likes *seeing* him naked because he's under the impression he has the body of a Greek God. Tyler learned within seven seconds of meeting my mother that women will point and laugh at him when he's naked. Tyler has been in love with my mother ever since.

"Seriously, bro. We need to make a list. I'm tired of seeing you moping around on your period every single day. You have the most epic job in the history of the world, and that alone should make you happy, but I get it. You need the girl. We'll get you the girl,"

Tyler reassures me as he rummages through the junk drawer in my kitchen for a piece of paper and a pen.

"How's a list going to help Charlotte fall in love with me?" I question him as he finds what he's looking for. He smoothes out a crumpled piece of paper on my countertop and writes in big, bold letters across the top: **How to Make Charlotte Bang Me.**

"That is so not the purpose of this. I don't want her to bang me," I complain.

Tyler stares at me with one eyebrow raised.

"Okay, fine!" I relent after a few seconds of his stare-down. "That's not the ONLY purpose. I can't just come right out and tell her I love her; she'll have a heart attack. We've known each other since birth and this is going to come out of left field. I need to figure out a way to ease her into it."

Tyler sighs in annoyance and crosses out the last part of the title and scribbles on the paper again. He turns it around to show me.

How to Make Charlotte ~~*Bang Me*~~ *Love Me. And Turn into a Giant Pussy.*

"You're such a dick."

Tyler shrugs. "Whatev. You're still a pussy. Okay, item number one ..."

He pauses, tapping the end of the pen against his chin while he thinks.

"Ooooh, I've got it! Show her your penis," he says aloud as he writes on the paper.

"What?! No! That is not going on the list," I argue as I try to take the page from him.

He jerks away, rolling his eyes at me.

"This is absolutely going on the list. Chicks need to test out the merchandise before they can make a decision. Do you honestly think she's going to love you if she thinks you might be harboring a pinky-peen in your pants?"

There's really no use in arguing with him at this point. Tyler is going to do whatever the fuck he wants. It's best to just humor him. It's not like I'm ever going to really use the list so who cares?

"Fine. But it's not going as number one."

Tyler smiles in victory and crosses out what he wrote, moving further down the page and rewriting it with a number five in front of it.

"There. Not at the top, not at the bottom. It will give you plenty of time to work up to the showing of the penis and then plenty of time to recover after you show it to her and she starts rocking back and forth in the corner, weeping silently."

Reaching across the counter, I punch him as hard as I can in the arm.

"Fucker! I bruise easily! What would Claire say if I told her you were abusing me?" Tyler questions as he rubs the spot on his arm where my fist connected.

"Shut up about my mother."

"No can do. She's going to be mine one day. You should just start calling me dad now," he says nonchalantly.

Ever since the day he met my mother—naked—he's been in love with her. For seven years I've had to endure him leering at her, making inappropriate comments, and imagining all the different ways my dad could die so he could console the grieving widow.

"I'm going to punch you right in the ball sack if you don't shut up," I warn him.

"Don't take that tone with me, young man."

I decide against beating the shit out of Tyler at this time. The faster he makes this stupid list, the faster he'll go home—to his parents' basement where he currently lives. No, I'm not kidding. He's a walking, talking epitome of a guy that refuses to grow up. He has a bachelor's degree in Japanese studies (a surefire way that he will never get a real job), works part-time at The Gap, and has never had a serious relationship.

Remind me again why I'm even thinking of taking advice from him?

"Okay, I've got a better idea for number one. Go shopping with her."

He writes out his new number one while I stare at him questioningly. When he looks up after writing it down, he stares at me like I'm an idiot.

"Bro, chicks love shopping. If you go and *ooh* and *ahh* over every pair of shoes she picks up, you'll be in her pants by the time you get to Auntie Anne's Pretzels," he informs me.

I don't even bother explaining to him, yet again, that my main purpose in life isn't to get in Charlotte's pants. Sure, it's something I dream about. Well, wet dream about. And the reason for my earlier Google search, but it's not the ultimate goal. I want her to love me. I want her to see me as something other than a friend. I

12

want her to realize that we're soul mates.

Fuck. Maybe I am getting my period.

"Alright, item number two. Take her to The Cheesecake Factory," he states as he continues to write.

"Why The Cheesecake Factory?"

Tyler shrugs as he taps the pen against the counter. "Chicks dig The Cheesecake Factory. It will show her that you can be all fancy and shit. Oooooh, oooooh, oooooh! Tell her she can order whatever she wants. That's a total cool-guy move," he tells me excitedly.

Alright, so this isn't too bad. I can handle a day of shopping as long as I'm with Charlotte. And The Cheesecake Factory is delicious.

"What else?" I ask as I go around the counter and stand next to him as he writes furiously.

"Dude, this is going to be epic. I am such a fucking genius. You better name your first born after me or something," he tells me as he continues making the list, quickly coming up with ten things that he swears will have Charlotte in love with me by the time I finish all of them. We work together, crossing things out and moving them around until we have a pretty good list of things for me to do to win Charlotte over.

I know I'm going to regret this. Somehow, some way, this is all going to come back and bite me in the ass, but I'm desperate. I know I'm a chickenshit and should just come right out and tell her, but that's not happening. This needs to be handled delicately. Tyler is the only person who knows how I feel about Charlotte. If anyone finds out about this before I'm ready … Well, let's just say having my mom tell my eighth grade English teacher at conferences that when I was little I used to walk around telling strangers my dad had a huge wiener will seem like the best day of my life.

Yep, totally going to regret this.

Chapter 2

- Hold Her Hair When She Pukes -

Charlotte graduated from college a few weeks ago. She had a few make-up classes to do during the summer session, but she's finally finished. She majored in Communications at Ohio State University, my alma mater. Today, her parents are throwing her a small graduation party at their home, and I can't deny the fact that I'm a little bit excited to get started on *The List*. After several six-packs of beer last night, this idea became more and more awesome. I mean seriously, what woman wouldn't love it if a guy started doing a shit ton of awesome things to prove to her how much he cares? And these aren't just everyday, common sense things like buying her flowers. These are the things women *want* men to do, but never come right out and ask for. I'm going to be a God among men when this is all said and done.

"Alright, bro. Are you ready for phase one? I mean, it will probably take a little while since it's early in the day, but you got this," Tyler reassures me as we get out of my car. I cock my head from side to side to crack my neck and shake out my hands.

"I can do this. I can TOTALLY do this. Phase one to commence by 9 pm," I reply.

Tyler gives me a high five and we make our way around to the backyard of Aunt Liz and Uncle Jim's house. My ears are immediately assaulted with the sounds of very bad, very off-pitch singing. Glancing under the tent they have set up, I see my Uncle Drew and Aunt Jenny doing karaoke. They're singing Sonny and Cher's "I Got You Babe," but they've changed up the lyrics just a bit.

"I'VE GOT YOU, BITCH!"

"I'VE GOT YOU, ASS!"

In case you've never met my Uncle Drew and Aunt Jenny, let me just tell you that this is pretty typical behavior. To put it nicely, they are bat shit crazy. Not crazy like *One Flew Over the Cuckoo's Nest,* crazy like ... I don't know, picture the most insane porno you've ever seen and then add in an episode from the Cooking Network with a couple of Oompa Loompas watching and you have a day in the life of Drew and Jenny Parritt. Uncle Drew is completely inappropriate one hundred percent of the time, and Aunt Jenny is a few fries short of a Happy Meal.

There's an awful, screeching feedback from the speakers as they stand facing one another, screaming into the microphones, and I wince as my mom greets me with a kiss on the cheek.

"Save me. Please, with all that is holy, save me. Get up there and sing something in tune." Her face is contorted in pain as Aunt Jenny continues to screech.

I used to sing in a band in high school. I'm not going to brag or anything, but I was pretty good. The band, not so much. I only joined the band to impress Charlotte because she made a comment once about how guys in a band are "so hot." Our one and only gig, was at Keystone Point Senior Center's annual Christmas party—I know, contain your excitement—and after we finished our set that consisted of a death metal version of "Silent Night" and a moving rendition of "Head Like a Hole" from Nine Inch Nails, I realized quickly that the whole band thing worked. Just not for me. Charlotte came running up on stage, flew right past me, and into the arms of the base player. It turns out guys that are in a band *who play the guitar* are "so hot." And that was our only gig because we were asked not so nicely to never play in public ever again.

Standing in the middle of the stage clutching my microphone, I tried not to throw it right at DJ's head as he lifted Charlotte up in the air and she wrapped her legs around his waist.

"You looked so hot playing that guitar!" Charlotte gushed as she peppered DJ's cheeks with kisses.

DJ looks over Charlotte's shoulder and smirks at me. Before I knew what was happening, the microphone sailed through the air, slamming against the back wall and barely missing DJ's face.

"Dude, what the fuck?" DJ shouted as he set Charlotte down on her feet and looked behind him at the dent that was now in the wall and the microphone rolling to a stop on the ground.

"Uh, it slipped." I shrugged.

Charlotte looked back and forth between us before calmly walking over to the back wall and scooping up the microphone. She turned and brought it over to me.

"Are you mad about something?"

I'm mad that you don't think singers are totally hot!

I took the microphone from her hand, trying not to look like an idiot when I felt her fingers brush against mine. "Nope. Not mad at all. I'm perfectly fine."

"Is this part of the show? Can I throw something? I want to throw a speaker," one of the old people in the front row said to a nurse.

"I don't want to eat peas for dinner anymore!" an old guy piped up from the back row, getting up from his wheelchair and kicking one of the tires.

Uh-oh.

"Sorry, folks! That wasn't part of the show. How about we play some Jingle Bells next?" I asked the crowd hopefully.

"SCREW JINGLE BELLS! AND SCREW BINGO! BINGO IS A SHITTY GAME!" a lady in front of the stage screamed.

Before I knew what was happening, thirty old people were getting up out of their chairs and wheelchairs and chanting

"BINGO SUCKS," advancing on the nursing staff.

DJ came up next to me and whispered in my ear while we watched the chaos unfold in front of us. "Dude, I think we should make a run for it."

"It will be fine. Let's just play something low-key to settle them down."

DJ quickly started strumming the first few bars to Silent Night and suddenly thirty pairs of cataract eyes turned in our direction. "NO! WE WANNA HEAR METALLICA!"

DJ immediately stopped playing and clutched on to Charlotte's arm as the group of blue hairs started advancing toward the stage.

"Oh Jesus. Forget the equipment. RUN!" I screamed.

"Maybe if you're lucky I'll sing a song or two later," I say with a sympathetic smile as Aunt Jenny butchers the words some more. I haven't sang on stage since that dark day at Keystone Point, but I'm all for doing whatever I can to help my mom out.

"I guess that's Joe, we don't have pot, but at least I'm sure of allllllll the snot."

"Hey there, Claire. You're looking especially lovely today," Tyler says as he leans in with his lips puckered for a kiss.

My mom holds her hand up in front of her, and Tyler's face is smooshed against her palm. She's only five foot four and a hundred and five pounds soaking wet. Tyler towers over her at around six foot, but she will kick anyone's ass if they piss her off.

"Stop calling me Claire or I will neuter you."

Tyler pulls back with a huge smile on his face and shoves his hands in his pockets.

"I look forward to our time together, honey."

"Make him stop," mom deadpans.

"Tyler, stop."

Tyler sighs happily and continues to smile at my mom until she finally shakes her head in annoyance and walks away.

"What is wrong with you?"

Tyler shrugs. "I can't help it. Every time I look at her, all I can think about is sex."

"I'm very uncomfortable with this conversation right now," I complain.

"It's your fault for marketing a dildo called *The Claire*."

I shudder and grab him by the arm, dragging him over to a table where my dad and Uncle Jim are sitting. "That thing was invented when I was six. You can't hold me responsible for that."

It's true. My company manufactures sex toys named after each female member of my family: *The Claire*, *The Liz*, and *The Jenny*. Do you have any idea how disturbing it is that the highest grossing product for the last eighteen years is one named after my mom? I have to read daily emails from customers that say things like, "*Claire* is the only one that can get me off," and "I was able to have multiple orgasms with *Claire*!" and "My wife screams *Claire* when she orgasms, and I'm perfectly fine with that!"

I want to puke just thinking about it.

"Hey, Uncle Jim, Dad, what's going on?" I ask as we walk up to the picnic table where they're sitting.

My dad and Uncle Drew met Uncle Jim ages ago when their job transferred them to another city. Uncle Jim had worked for the same company for a few years and was in charge of showing my dad and Uncle Drew the ropes on their first day. Uncle Jim invited them over for dinner that first night and they've been friends ever since. My dad and Uncle Jim are a lot alike. They have the same sense of humor and are great family men. They used to look similar when they were younger, but my dad has definitely aged more gracefully. Or should I say not aged at all. He's like Dick Clark. You know, before the whole dying thing.

My dad still works out regularly and stays in great shape. There isn't one gray hair on his head. Uncle Jim is tall and lean, and I'm pretty sure has never worked out a day in his life. The guys like to tease him about how he should dye his brown hair since it's started graying at the temples, but Aunt Liz always puts her foot down. She says it makes him look sophisticated. I think she just tells him that so he doesn't cry himself to sleep at night.

"Your Aunt Liz said you guys had a great production meeting the other day. Something about a contest you decided to do to name the new sex toy?" Uncle Jim asks.

"You should name it *The Beaver Banger*. Or *The Tyler Tickler*," Tyler says with a laugh.

"Tyler, you get more and more annoying every time I see

you," Dad says with a shake of his head.

"Thank you, sir! How's your cholesterol? Can I get you something fried and dipped in butter?" Tyler asks as he takes a seat across from him.

"Stop trying to kill me off Tyler or I'm going to shove my foot up your ass."

"Very good, sir!" Tyler nods.

I hear a commotion over by the deck and all the breath leaves my lungs when I turn and see the sliding glass door open and Charlotte step outside.

She's wearing a pale yellow strapless dress, and with her hair up in a ponytail, I can see so much of her sun kissed skin that I unconsciously lick my lips.

We should have put "lick her skin" on the list. It wouldn't be weird at all if I just walked up to her and ran my tongue across her shoulder, would it? I could tell her she had a piece of food there or something. Totally normal.

Our eyes meet across the yard and a huge smile lights up her face. She squeals and comes running down the stairs of the deck in my direction. I can't keep the excitement from my face as I start walking to meet her halfway.

When she's a few feet away, I start to lift my arms to grab her in a hug.

"Hey, Gavin," she says as an afterthought, running right past me and throwing herself into Rocco's arms.

Rocco, who's standing right behind me and I hadn't even noticed.

Dejected, I stand there and watch as he swings her around in his arms and peppers her face with kisses.

Fucking Rocco.

I walk back over to the table and stand behind my dad and Uncle Jim. While I'm busy trying not to throw up in my mouth from the PDA going on right in front of me, let me tell you a little bit about Rocco. Charlotte met Rocco three months ago at her sorority mixer. Rocco is a year younger than her and had just pledged the brother house of her sorority. Rocco has blonde hair that he regularly gets highlighted. Rocco always wears khakis and pastel-colored polo shirts with the collar popped and loafers without socks. No, I'm not kidding. I met Rocco once and I wasn't impressed. This is the first boyfriend Charlotte has had that lasted longer than a few weeks and therefore, I want to kill Rocco. Today is the first time the family is meeting Rocco, so I'm hoping everyone else will see that there is something wrong with this guy. He probably seems okay to you right now: nice hair, swanky dresser, and member of a fraternity. But just wait. You'll see what I'm talking about.

"Oh, sweetheart, it's been too long! We should never spend this much time apart ever again. I had to watch the last two new episodes of *The Kardashians* all by myself," Rocco complains with a pout as he sets Charlotte back down on her feet.

Charlotte laughs a little uncomfortably and I watch as she pinches him in the arm and he shoots her a dirty look. I doubt anyone else notices that little exchange, but I do because I'm obsessed with everything she does.

"Did I say *The Kardashians*? I totally meant … football. I had to watch FOOTBALL all by myself."

She grabs Rocco's hand, turning him to face Uncle Jim.

"Dad, this is my boyfriend, Rocco. Rocco, this is my dad, Jim Gilmore."

Uncle Jim stands up and extends his hand out to Rocco. Rocco ignores the hand and throws both of his arms around Uncle Jim and squeezes him in a hug that lasts entirely too long by the uncomfortable look on Uncle Jim's face.

"Charlie has told me so much about you! Can I call you *Dad*? It's okay if I call you *Dad*, right?" Rocco asks excitedly as he finally lets go of Uncle Jim and steps back to Charlotte's side.

"If you call me *Dad* I will chop off your dick and leave you for dead on the side of the road," Uncle Jim states before sitting back down.

"Oh, Charlie, you were right! Your dad is quite the character! I already feel like part of the family. Dad, you have a lovely home," Rocco gushes as he wraps his arm around Charlotte's waist.

"Someone get me my shotgun," Uncle Jim mutters to himself.

"What's up, fuckers?" Uncle Drew asks as he walks up to the table. "What song should Jenny and I sing next, any requests?"

Rocco raises his hand excitedly. "Oooooh, I've got one! Do you know the words to 'Don't Rain on my Parade?' I love me some Barbara-OUCH!"

Rocco's hand flies to his ribs after Charlotte elbows him.

"I'm like, totally kidding, dudes. It would be some epic shit if you could sing Megadeth," Rocco adds in a weird, deep voice.

"Who is this tool?" Drew whispers in my ear.

"He's Charlotte's boyfriend. She met him at school," I whisper back as Rocco starts banging his head and attempting to sing death metal.

"What school did he go to, Closet State?" Drew mutters.

"Can I get you something to drink?" Charlotte asks Rocco, interrupting his singing.

"I would KILL for a white wine spritzer, sweetie. I'm so parched," Rocco informs her as they walk away, hand-in-hand toward the row of coolers back by the deck.

"What the fuck just happened here?" Uncle Jim asks as he watches the two of them walk away.

"I think your daughter is dating the president of Cum Guzzlers University," Drew informs him.

"I'm going to need Tequila for this," Jim tells us with a sad shake of his head.

Three hours later, we're all sitting on the deck listening to Rocco tell the story of how he met Charlotte.

"And she had on a pair of the CUTEST shoes I've ever seen. They were black with white polka dots and had a little pink bow right above the kitten heel. I knew I just HAD to meet this woman."

Charlotte is sitting in between Rocco and me on a bench seat, and the only thing stopping me from throwing a temper tantrum in the middle of the deck is the feel of her leg rubbing up against mine every few minutes when she shifts positions. I watch as she brings a hand up to her forehead and rubs it with her fingertips, like she's getting a headache.

"Okay, by my count, she's had five glasses of wine. I think it's time to put *The List* in motion," Tyler whispers in my ear from the other side of me. "Ask her if she feels okay."

Giving him a slight nod, I lean closer to Charlotte and whisper right by her ear.

"Are you feeling okay? Do you want me to get you some water?" I ask her.

I feel Tyler flick my shoulder, and I know I shouldn't have asked her about water. The point is for her to throw up so I can be all gentlemanly and hold her hair back while she pukes. I don't want her to feel like shit if it isn't necessary.

Charlotte turns her face to mine, and I can feel her warm breath against my lips.

"Thanks, I'm good. Just think I had a few too many glasses of wine. They're starting to churn in my stomach."

Churning stomach equals puking! It's going to happen! It's totally going to happen!

She turns away from me and leans forward, resting her elbows on her knees while Rocco continues to talk about shoes and how Charlotte's lip gloss perfectly matched her dress.

I need to take action. Right the fuck now! Puking can happen at any time, without any warning. I need to be prepared. I NEED TO BE PREPARED, DAMMIT!

I quickly reach out and wrap the long ponytail hanging over her shoulder in my hand, pulling it back away from her face. In my excitement to be awesome though, I pull a little too hard and yank her head up.

"Ouch! What the hell? Did you just pull my hair?"

While she questions me, everyone on the deck suddenly turns their eyes in our direction and all conversation stops. And here's where I turn into a fucking moron. I can't let go of her hair. The silky strands are wrapped around my fingers, and it's like my hand has a mind of its own and won't let go. I squeeze tighter and pull harder, and this is now turning into a nightmare because she's glaring at me, not giving me the look of love I imagined when I saved her from puke-hair.

"Dude, too soon. Too soon! Abort!" Tyler whispers frantically in my ear.

"Ooooh, Gavin likes to pull hair. Kinky!" Uncle Drew says with a satisfied nod as he stares at me.

"I like having my hair pulled. Why haven't you pulled my hair lately, Drew?" Jenny questions.

Let go of her hair! Let go of her fucking hair, douche!

"Jesus, let go or say something!" Tyler whispers again.

I mutter the first thing that comes to mind as I continue to hold her ponytail in my hand.

"Your hair is soft. Did you switch conditioners?"

"Oh sweet Jesus," Tyler mutters.

"Seriously, Drew. Why haven't you pulled my hair during sex lately? My hair isn't soft enough for you, is it? Charlotte, what conditioner do you use?" Jenny asks.

"She uses Aveda moisturizing conditioner. I can get you some free samples from my stylist, Jenny," Rocco tells her.

"Can you let go, please?" Charlotte asks me softly.

"You shouldn't have puke-hair. Wine puke doesn't wash out easily. I use Herbal Essence and it smells like strawberries," I mumble.

All of the beer I've consumed under the blazing sun this afternoon, mixed with my mortification that I still haven't let go of Charlotte's hair, is starting to make me feel queasy.

"Drew, pull my hair," Jenny demands.

"Babe, I can't pull your hair. Pulling your hair makes me want to have sex with you. I pulled a hammy last night when we were on the swing set, remember?" Drew complains.

"Drew, seriously. Over share," my mom complains with a roll of her eyes.

"Should I escort him out for you, Claire?" Tyler asks my mom in a concerned voice.

Oh Jesus, here it comes. I'm going to puke.

Finally letting go of Charlotte's hair, I jump up from my seat and run down the stairs of the deck, over to the bushes on the side of the house, and empty my stomach of beer and shame.

A few seconds later, I feel a hand patting me on my back as I heave. When I feel comfortable that no more vomit is going to come out, I stand up and turn around.

"Are you done, or is there more? Want me to hold your hair back?" Tyler asks with a laugh.

Chapter 3

- Make Her Jealous -

"How about some ginger ale? Or some dry toast? Maybe I should take your temperature," mom says as she fusses over me and feels my forehead.

My mom and I have always been unusually close. And no, I'm not talking Norman Bates and his mom close. That's just sick. I think it's because she was a single mother for the first four years of my life. Or it could be that when I was little she used to joke all the time about how she hated kids. I think sometimes she overcompensates trying to make up for all of those jokes by doting on me now that I'm an adult.

"Mom, I'm fine. Really. It was probably just something I ate." The lie easily flows from my mouth as I swat her hand away from my head.

"I'm actually not feeling so hot myself, Claire. I could

use a sponge bath," Tyler tells her.

"How about I take your temperature with a rectal thermometer the size of my fist?" Mom threatens.

"I'm strangely aroused right now," Tyler muses.

"Do you want me to throw up again?" I ask him angrily with a punch to his arm.

After my awesome projectile vomiting skills in the shrubbery, the party had started to disperse and Charlotte left with Rocco to go to dinner, explaining she would have invited me to come but she was afraid I might be contagious and she didn't want to get sick.

Super. Now she thinks I'm a leper.

We're sitting in Liz and Jim's kitchen while everyone else is outside cleaning up. I had come in here to get some peace and quiet and to get away from Uncle Drew so he would stop asking me if I could puke on command because he was sad he missed the show, and my mom and Tyler followed me in here to check on me. My mortification level is at an ultimate high right now. There's nothing else that could possibly make this day any worse.

"You know, if you want Charlotte to realize you're in love with her, pulling her hair and throwing up in her parents' bushes probably wasn't the best idea," Mom informs me.

I take that back. THIS could possibly make my day worse. Much worse.

"Oh my gosh, what?! What are you talking about? I'm not in love with Charlotte. You're insane. Where would you get that idea? That's just crazy. It's nonsense. Preposterous! She's like my sister. We used to take baths together."

If you ramble enough, people will think what you're saying is true, right?

"Yes, and you used to stand up in the middle of the tub and say, 'Hey, Charlotte, look at my big wiener!' I hope that's not what your next plan of attack is," Mom says with a serious look on her face.

Note to self: remove number five from The List.

"I'm not going to show her my wiener!"

"I really think you should show her your wiener. I'm not taking it off of the list," Tyler adds.

Everyone needs to stop saying wiener right the fuck now!

"Did someone say wiener? What list? What's everyone talking about?" Aunt Liz asks as she walks into the kitchen with an armful of dirty dishes that she piles in the sink.

"A list to get Charlotte to realize Gavin's in love with her," Tyler tells her.

"Dude! Shut the fuck up!" I yell.

"Oh thank God. It's about time you do something about it. I thought your mother and I were going to be old and gray before you manned the fuck up," Aunt Liz says as she walks over to the table and takes a seat next to my mom.

My mom and Aunt Liz have been best friends for all my life and for a lot of years before that. They've been through everything together, and sometimes I think they share a brain. It's hard to believe they aren't sisters with the way they fight. They talk more shit to each other than a book with "your mother is so fat" jokes in it.

"I think I'm going to wear blue to the wedding. I saw this

33

gorgeous dress on sale at Macy's the other day. I think I have a coupon," Mom tells Liz.

"Oh hell no! I already told you I was going to wear blue, you whore. You can't wear the same color as me, that's tacky," Liz complains.

Oh my God, this is not happening right now.

"Fuck your mother. I'm wearing blue. I already found my dress," Mom argues.

"I'm the mother of the bride. The mother of the fucking bride! That means it's up to me!" Liz fires back.

"Claire, I think you would look lovely in blue," Tyler pipes in.

Mom turns to face Tyler and folds her arms on top of the table. "When I'm finished neutering you, I'm going to take your tiny little neuticles and light them on fire."

Putting my elbows on the table and my head in my hands, I try to tune out the conversation going on around me. How in the hell do my mom and Liz know I'm in love with Charlotte? How is this possible? And if they know, does Charlotte know? She can't know. There's no way.

"You should probably take hair pulling off of the list. Charlotte never even liked it when I brushed her hair when she was little. She has a sensitive head," Liz informs me.

"You should buy her flowers."

"Or jewelry. Women love getting jewelry."

"I never cared much for jewelry. I was happy if he just remembered to put the toilet seat down."

"True. Put down the toilet seat. Ooooh, make her a mix tape!

Those are always fun."

"Nineteen-eighty-five called, they want their idea back."

"Suck my dick."

"This is better than watching porn," Tyler whispers in awe as my mom and Liz go back and forth.

"Can we all just stop talking about this right now? I am not in love with her, I'm not making her a mix tape, and we're not getting married," I tell them, finally looking up from the table.

"You're not in love with who? Are you dating someone now?"

Whipping around in my chair, I see Charlotte standing in the kitchen doorway with a look of horror on her face. Of course all of the idiots in the room with me choose NOW to not say anything, and the silence drags on for so long that I feel like I might puke again.

"Gavin? Are you seeing someone?" she asks again.

I should just tell her now. Tell her that there could never possibly be anyone else because I've been in love with her since I was six. Tell her that she's beautiful and sweet and amazing and I want to spend the rest of my life loving her.

But I don't. I sit here with my mouth open like a tool.

"Dude, didn't he tell you? He met this totally hot chick at a bar a few weeks ago. Seriously, we're talking super model hot. And she used to be a gymnast so she's real bendy. Nice girl. Huge rack."

I don't know what the fuck Tyler is saying right now, and I can't even do anything to stop him because I'm frozen in my seat. Charlotte looks like I did an hour ago when I jumped up and ran off the deck. She looks sick to her stomach and like she might cry at any second. She's probably completely disgusted with me right now. I pulled her hair, puked in her lawn, and now I'm dating a pretend woman with big boobs.

"What are you doing back so soon? I thought you and Rocco were going to dinner," Aunt Liz asks, and Charlotte finally looks away from me and goes over to the sink to pour herself a glass of water.

"We just got something quick. One of his friends called when we were finishing up and asked him to go shoe shopping, so I just had him drop me off," Charlotte tells her as she polishes off her water and puts the glass in the sink.

"I'm sorry, did you just say your boyfriend ditched you to go shoe shopping?" my mom asks her.

Charlotte sighs and crosses her arms in front of her. "He didn't ditch me. I told him he could go because I was tired."

"You don't really mean shoe shopping right? You meant to say shopping for sports equipment or a new surround sound system, right?" Aunt Liz asks.

"He told us his favorite book of all time was *Under the Rainbow: The Real Liza Minnelli*. I'm pretty sure shoe shopping would be right up his alley," Mom reminds her.

"Has Rocco gotten the memo yet that he's gay?" Aunt Liz questions her.

Tyler starts laughing hysterically and reaches his hand up to fist-bump my aunt.

"Seriously, Mom? Are you judging him? That's really low," Charlotte complains.

"I'm not judging him. Some of the best people I've ever met are gay. I just don't particularly want my daughter dating someone who's gay."

Charlotte stomps her foot and growls at Liz, and I have to tell myself not to get too excited. I love seeing her get fired up. Her cheeks turn pink and her eyes sparkle. Now is NOT the time to get a boner.

"He is NOT gay! He's just … he's in touch with his feminine side."

Tyler snorts and Charlotte shoots an angry look in his direction.

"Honey, he doesn't have a feminine side. He has a vagina," Aunt Liz informs her.

Before Charlotte can go completely ape shit on her mother, a loud banging sound comes from the living room followed by a bunch of cursing. A few seconds later, Aunt Jenny walks in with a scowl on her face.

"You really need to get that French door to the backyard fixed, Liz. All the humility has made it stick and it doesn't open very easily."

"Ahhhh yes, the *humility* in the air. We've humbled the door into not opening for people," Aunt Liz replies.

"I'm going to bed. Gavin, don't forget we're all going out tomorrow night. Make sure to invite this new girlfriend of yours so I can meet her," Charlotte says as she walks behind me and pats me on the shoulder before she leaves the room.

I hold my breath until I hear the click of her heels taper off down the hallway and the door to her bedroom close.

Turning around in my seat, I smack Tyler in the arm once again.

"Owww! What the fuck was that for?!"

"Girlfriend? Supermodel hot? Bendy?" I whisper through clenched teeth.

"The bendy part was a bit overkill, but it totally worked. She was insanely jealous," Aunt Liz says with a nod of her head.

She wasn't jealous. We're friends. Best friends. She's irritated because she found out about it from Tyler in a room full of people instead of directly from me. When she started dating Rocco, she sat me down and told me, just like a good friend does. I should have taken her aside alone and told her about my girlfriend.

Oh my God, what the fuck am I saying? I don't have a girlfriend!

"Gavin, you have a girlfriend?! Oh my gosh that's so exciting! I have condoms in my purse if you need them. They're the kind with insecticide so they totally work," Aunt Jenny tells me.

"*Spermicide*, Jenny. Spermicide. Sweet Jesus," Aunt Liz complains.

"Gavin's cock has roaches, pass it on!" Tyler laughs.

"It's all fun and games until you assholes start talking about my son having sex. Gavin doesn't need condoms," Mom informs everyone.

"Are you ready to be Nana Claire right now? Because I'm too young and pretty to be Gammy Liz. If he's going to be having sex with my daughter, he will damn well wrap his shit up!" Aunt Liz yells. "Jenny, give him your condoms."

Aunt Jenny starts to walk over to the counter where her purse sits but stops when my mom speaks.

"Jenny, you take one more step in that direction and I will rip out your ovaries," Mom threatens.

Aunt Jenny freezes again and holds her hands up in the air like she's under arrest.

"Throwing away all of the condoms you found in his top dresser drawer didn't stop him from having sex with Shelly Collins in the twelfth grade. Quit being a twat and let him have the damn condoms," Aunt Liz adds with a roll of her eyes.

You know, sometimes I think I'd like it better if my mom had absolutely no friends at all. Especially friends that she tells everything to and that also happens to be the mother of the woman I'm in love with. Talking about my one and only sexual encounter on prom night that only happened because I found out Charlotte lost her virginity the week before to the bass player in my band obviously wasn't my finest hour. And the fact that my mom and Aunt Liz have already picked out their grandparent names is disturbing. Gammy Liz???

"We are never to speak again of my son having sex. EVER!" Mom warns.

"Thank you," I mutter gratefully with a sigh.

"Instead, we should be talking about what his girlfriend will be wearing tomorrow night," she states.

Oh my God.

"Make sure she wears something totally slutty," Aunt Liz tells me.

"And make sure you watch Charlotte out of the corner of your eye so you can see the look on her face," Mom adds.

"Um, are we forgetting something here? I don't have a girlfriend," I remind them.

"I got your back, bro. I've got the perfect woman for you," Tyler tells me.

"You don't know any women. You only know hookers. You are not setting my son up on a fake date with a hooker." Mom glares at him and practically growls.

"Hey, that was one time and it was an honest mistake. She was right outside the bar asking people if they wanted to go on a date. Who turns down an offer like that?" Tyler asks.

"Someone who doesn't want to get VD," Mom tells him.

"I had Chlamydia once. It wasn't so bad. Antibiotics cleared it right up," Jenny says, still standing by the counter with her arms up in the air.

"Tyler, I am trusting you to find my son a nice girl that you DO NOT have to pay."

Tyler salutes her and then rests his hand over his heart.

"Your wish is my command, my beauty. Is there anything else I can do for you on this fine evening?"

Mom rubs her temples with her fingers and starts muttering under her breath about cyanide tablets and firing squads while Aunt Liz and Tyler discuss the girl he's going to hook me up with tomorrow night.

I was really looking forward to a night out with my friends, even if I have to suffer through more hours of watching Charlotte with Rocco—her flamboyantly annoying boyfriend. Now, I'm pretty sure I should just plan on leaving the country and changing my name. It would be less trouble.

"Meet me outside by your car in fifteen minutes. I'll slip you the condoms when your mom isn't looking," Aunt Jenny whispers in my ear. "Just make sure you don't use them with apple butter and grapeseed oil. It sounds like a good idea, but it's not. Trust me."

Chapter 4

— Make Her Think You're a Sex God —

"Can you get me the notes from last week's interactive design meeting? Also, book the conference room on the sixth floor for tomorrow morning at nine. We have those fifteen product testers coming in to give their opinions on the orange dreamsicle flavored massage lotion," I distractedly tell Ava as I sort through my emails.

Ava is Charlotte's sister and a year younger than her. Liz decided that her daughter should do something other than get spray tans and take naps on her summer break from school so she made her take an internship at Seduction and Snacks and work as my assistant. Charlotte and Ava share physical attributes. Just like Charlotte, Ava is slender with long dark hair, but that's where the similarities end. Where Charlotte is sweet, funny, thoughtful, and amazing, Ava is … not. She's pretty much just a bitch. Charlotte and I used to argue a lot when we were younger, but Ava and I would get into all-out brawls. Punches were thrown, things were lit on fire … it was anarchy.

I look up after a few minutes when she hasn't answered me and see her standing there pressing buttons on her iPad, concentrating furiously.

"Ava, did you hear me?"

She sighs in annoyance but still doesn't look up from the screen. "Yes, I heard you. Book the fifteenth floor and make notes about massages."

Ava is the worst assistant on the face of the earth. And I can't even say she means well because she doesn't. She couldn't care less about this job.

"Ava, you have an iPad in your hand for notes. Did you even type anything I said?" I ask her in annoyance.

I don't have time for this crap. I have a ton of work to do and an illness to fake before seven o'clock tonight.

"Oh my GOD this is so hard. I just can't do this," Ava whines and stomps her foot just like her sister. Except when Charlotte does it, I don't want to hurl myself across my desk and strangle her.

"It's okay, I know it's a lot to take in at once. Just take good notes and you'll be fine," I reassure her.

"Uuuughhhh! I don't understand how anyone passes level thirty-five of Candy Crush," she complains, still tapping away at her iPad.

I don't even bother replying to her. I just lean forward and bang my head against the top of my desk.

I'm still banging it a few minutes later when my phone starts ringing. After five rings, I lift my head and stare at Ava.

"Are you going to answer that phone or what?" she asks in annoyance.

I will not strangle her. I will not strangle her.

"Creative Development, this is Gavin," I say into the phone as Ava turns and walks out of my office without ever looking up from her iPad.

"You sound like a douche bag. Don't answer the phone like that," Tyler tells me.

"Shut up. What do you want?"

"Seriously, you should answer it 'Dicks for Chicks, how can I help you?'"

I ignore Tyler's suggestion and quickly close out my email when I see a customer comment about how "Claire can be taken up the ass."

"I'm bringing your girlfriend to the bar at six-thirty. We'll meet you in the parking lot so make sure you wear something pretty," he tells me.

"Actually, I think I'm coming down with something. I'm not feeling so hot."

I cough a few times into the phone to make it sound real.

"Suck it, dick nose. You're going tonight," Tyler states.

He doesn't even give me a chance to plead my case before he hangs up on me and I hear the dial tone in my ear.

"Son of a bitch," I mutter as I put the receiver back.

"Hey, Gavin, you want some coffee?" Ava yells from her desk right outside my door.

All right, maybe I've been too hard on her. I start to feel a little bad about getting irritated a few minutes ago. I'm nervous and frustrated about tonight. And what the hell am I supposed to do with a fake girlfriend? I'm probably taking it out on Ava just a little bit.

"Coffee sounds great," I yell back to her as I pull up my search engine and type in *twenty-four-hour illnesses that aren't contagious or make people think you're a leper.*

"Awesome. Can you get me a Venti nonfat double shot espresso while you're out?" Ava replies.

Abandoning my Google search, I smack my head against top of my desk and pray to God that tonight is better than today.

"I cannot BELIEVE you set me up with her. Of all the women in all the world, you had to pick *her.*"

I'm standing in the parking lot of Wolfey's, the bar we all frequent when we have something to celebrate. I had pulled in at the same time as Tyler and my "girlfriend" and watched in horror as she stepped out of his mom's car that he borrowed for the evening.

Right now she's checking out her reflection in my passenger

side window while I rip into Tyler.

"Dude, do you have any idea how hard it was to find a chick willing to pretend to be your girlfriend for the evening? This was the best I could do on short notice. What's wrong with her? She's hot," Tyler says as we both look over the hood of the car to find her staring at us.

"What's wrong with her is that I used to date her. And she's psychotic. Plus, my mom hates her. If she finds out I spent a night with *her*, even if it's pretend, she is going to lose her shit."

The *her* in question is Brooklyn Daniels. We went to school together from kindergarten through high school, and I dated her for exactly two weeks in eleventh grade. By day three I had met everyone in her family, including an aunt and uncle who flew in from Turks and Caicos just to meet me. By day ten she'd given me three photo albums filled with pictures of herself. No, not her and I together, just her. Pictures that to this day still burn my retinas when I think about them. Where was I? Oh, yes. By day eleven she'd tattooed my initials on her lower back, by day twelve she'd given me a wedding scrapbook filled with bridal magazine clippings of what she wanted our wedding to look like, and by day fourteen she'd suggested that we go to couple's counseling because she thought I didn't value her. By day sixty-eight she was history.

Yes, we only dated for two weeks, but it took fifty-two days after that for her to get the memo. Brooklyn Daniels is a stage five clinger. I almost had to move to get her to leave me alone. The only thing that worked was having my mom show up at her job at the local ice cream shop where she told Brooklyn that if she didn't leave me alone, she'd shove so many sugar cones up her ass that she'd be burping up chocolate and vanilla twist for the rest of her life.

"Can we go inside now? I need a drink."

Tyler and I continue to stare at her across the top of the car. She seems normal right now. Maybe things have changed and she's not bat shit crazy anymore. I mean, we all do stupid things in high school, right? She's twenty-five years old now. She's probably matured.

Brooklyn walks around the front of the car and comes up next to me, linking her arm through my elbow.

"It's nice to see you again, Gavin. So, what are we going for tonight? A little jealousy or total annihilation?"

"Jealousy."

"Make the bitch cry!" Tyler and I inform her at the same time.

"Well okay then. How about somewhere in the middle? Are you okay with that?" Brooklyn asks as we walk toward the door of Wolfey's.

"Nothing over the top. I just want Charlotte to get a tiny bit jealous and maybe see me differently."

"False. You need to make Charlotte think he's a sex God. So talk about his penis a lot," Tyler informs her.

Trying not to blush with embarrassment, I smack Tyler on the arm. "We do not have to follow the list exactly. No talking about my penis."

Brooklyn nods as Tyler opens the door for us. "Got it. No problem."

"I really appreciate you doing this for me, Brooklyn. I know we didn't end on the best of terms, and I apologize for my mom throwing chocolate sprinkles in your eye."

We make our way through the crowd of people to the back of the bar and the group of tables where the gang always sits.

"Really, it's fine. No hard feelings at all. That was a long time ago, and I'm a different person now."

I breathe a sigh of relief at her words and try not to be nervous when I see Charlotte standing next to Ava, staring right at us.

This is going to work. It's totally going to work.

THIS IS NOT WORKING AT ALL! CODE RED!

"Gavin, let's go into the bathroom so you can stick it in my ass again like last week. That was soooooooo good," Brooklyn slurs as she wraps her arms around my neck and drapes her body across my chest.

I try to shush her so she stops talking so loudly but that just makes it worse.

"GAVIN HAS AN AMAZING PENIS!" Brooklyn screams over the sounds of music and people.

For the most part tonight, no one has paid much attention to Brooklyn, which I think is part of the problem. She wants people to notice her. I just want her to sit next to me quietly and pretend to be a nice, sweet girlfriend. The first time I whispered that suggestion in her ear, she reached under the table and squeezed my nuts in a death grip. Obviously my recommendation wasn't pleasing to her ears.

Tyler, Ava, Charlotte, Rocco, Brooklyn, and myself have been here for exactly two hours. Within the first three minutes, Brooklyn has downed two dirty martinis and three shots of something called Liquid Marijuana. My sister Sophia couldn't make it tonight because she just started the summer session of her last year in college. I am thanking my lucky stars for that because she probably would have dragged Brooklyn by her hair into the bathroom and beat the shit out of her. Even though Sophia was only twelve when I dated Brooklyn, she still remembers. And she shares our mother's hatred of her.

Ava has been shooting her dirty looks all night, even before Brooklyn turned belligerent. I've seen her whispering in Charlotte's ear every time Brooklyn speaks, and I can only imagine what she's saying. Probably something along the lines of "I'd punch that bitch in the face if I wasn't afraid of breaking a nail or missing a text message when I had to put my phone down."

I wish Molly, Charlotte and Ava's youngest sister, was here. Molly is the peacekeeper in the family and can diffuse any situation. She probably would have been able to get Brooklyn to stop drinking eight shots ago with no problem. Unfortunately, Molly is only nineteen and therefore, not allowed in the bar. Same goes with both of Aunt Jenny and Uncle Drew's kids, Veronica, also nineteen, and Billy, sixteen. All they care about is being the life of the party and probably would be doing plenty of stupid things to take the focus off of Drunky McDrunkerson sitting here next to me.

"Dude, this plan is NOT working," I complain quietly to Tyler next to me.

"What are you talking about? It's totally working. Charlotte can't stand to see you with her."

"The entire bar can't stand to see me with her because she keeps yelling at random people that she's going to cut their mother," I complain.

"She'll be fine. Just make sure she takes her meds," Tyler tells me distractedly as he winks at a girl a few tables away.

"Meds? What meds? Should she be mixing medication with alcohol?" Panicking when I feel Brooklyn's head slump forward, I place my fingers against the side of her neck to make sure she's still alive.

Her head jerks up suddenly and she starts screaming. "OH MY GOD I LOVE THIS SONG! I WANT TO DANCE!"

I stare at her in horror as she laughs uncontrollably. She suddenly shoots up from her chair and points to a guy at the far end of the bar about twenty yards away. "Do you see that guy? He's staring at me. He's creepy and he keeps staring at me. That little Chinaman keeps staring."

Glancing over to where she points, I see nothing but a group of women talking to a fifty-something guy.

"I'm going to chase him," Brooklyn states.

"What? No. He's not staring at you and you aren't chasing anyone."

"I don't think that's a Chinaman. He looks Italian to me," Tyler muses, totally not helping the situation.

Brooklyn narrows her eyes at the poor unsuspecting man who isn't even facing our direction.

"Yep. This is totally happening. That little Vaginaman is going down."

Before I can stop her, she kicks her chair out of the way and goes running full sprint to the bar.

The guy she's aiming for looks up and sees her barreling toward him at full speed. A moment of panic flashes across his face before he slams his beer bottle down on the bar and takes off running in the opposite direction.

"RUN, VAGINAMAN, RUN!" Brooklyn screams as she runs after him. Everyone in the bar stares in shock and moves out of the way as she chases him right out the front door and into the parking lot.

I turn my head away from her and glare at Tyler who just shrugs. "Don't give me that look. She wasn't this cuckoo when I banged her a few months ago."

"Jesus Christ, you slept with her? What is wrong with you?" I scold.

"What? I like the crazy. Crazy chicks are needy and hot in bed. Don't worry, I'll go after her."

Tyler gets up from his seat and heads to the door. Out of the corner of my eye I see a flash of something and watch as the

Italian-China-vagina-man streaks past the window outside with Brooklyn right on his heels.

Looking across the table, I catch Charlotte's eye and she gives me a sympathetic smile. Obviously making her jealous didn't work. And I'm pretty sure hearing Brooklyn shout about anal all night long didn't convince her I'm a sex God. All this evening did was make her feel sorry for me. I wanted her to see me with another woman and realize she has feelings for me. If I ever need another fake girlfriend again, remind me to never put Tyler in charge of finding her.

"I caught the Chinaman. He won't be bothering me anymore. Show me your penis," Brooklyn suddenly demands next to my chair before collapsing onto my lap and dissolving into a fit of tears.

Chapter 5

- Take Her to The Cheesecake Factory -

Since Wolfey's the other night was a total bust, I'm moving down the list and forgetting all about it. Out of sight, out of mind. I know what you're thinking, I should just give up the list and come up with something else. Something like, oh, I don't know, just telling her the truth. Do you have any idea what it's like to be a dude and tell a woman you love her only to have her shoot you down? Neither do I, but I'm guessing it would cut me deep. Especially considering this is Charlotte we're talking about. It's not like I could just drop that bomb on her, walk away, and never see her again. Our families are practically related. I'll have to spend Christmas and birthdays with her while she looks at me with pity from across the room. Poor, lonely Gavin holding a torch for his best friend while she moves on, marries Rocco, and spends the rest of her life listening to Barbara Streisand and shoe shopping with him.

This list is my only hope of saving face. It has to work. So I'm moving on to one of my favorites on the list: take her to The Cheesecake Factory. Glancing down at my cell phone, I see a text from Tyler reminding me what to do.

Chicks love cool guys that order for them. Be cool, dude. Make sure she knows money is no object. Chicks dig it when guys say that.

"Hey, Gavin, sorry I'm late. Traffic was a bitch," Charlotte says brightly as she kisses me on the cheek and then rushes over to take her seat across from me.

It takes everything in me not to vault over the table and tackle her to the ground. I'm guessing that would be frowned upon at The Cheesecake Factory.

"It's fine. I haven't been here that long. How was job hunting today?" I ask as I signal for our waitress so she can get Charlotte something to drink.

"Job hunting sucks. I should have just stayed in college for the rest of my life," she says with a laugh as she looks over the drink menu. "How was work for you? I heard you're doing some new promotional thing where you're letting customers vote on a toy name. That sounds fun."

"The customers seem to like it so far. We've gotten some great submissions and some creepy ones," I tell her.

"Creepy ones?"

"Well, the creepy ones have all come from Tyler. I need to block him from the company website."

Charlotte laughs and I'm instantly hard. I try to think about something other than the musical sound of her laugh, like cheesecake. But that doesn't help; I love cheesecake. And now I'm thinking about smothering Charlotte's body with cheesecake and then licking it off. I wonder if she would taste better with cherry cheesecake or blueberry? Does blueberry sauce stain the skin? I bet Uncle Drew would know the answer to that ...

"I was asked to come to the grand opening of a new sex toy store in Cleveland this weekend. You should totally come. They want me to cut the ribbon during the opening ceremony," I explain.

"That sounds fun. I'll definitely be there. Just text me the address and when it is. Thanks for asking me to lunch too. I haven't been here in a while. Rocco brought me here on our first date and our bill was outrageous."

Fucking Rocco. I'll show him. My bill will be bigger than his bill.

"So how's Brooklyn?" Charlotte asks, checking a text on her phone and then setting it to the side of her silverware.

I don't know. How *is* Brooklyn? I haven't spoken to her since she passed out at the table and Tyler drove her home. I told him if he gave her my cell number or told her where I lived, I'd tell my mom he still sucks his thumb at night when he sleeps.

"She's great. Just great. Wonderful and great."

Charlotte leans forward and puts her elbows on the table while I gush about Brooklyn.

Holy cleavage, Batman. Don't look directly at the cleavage. Look at the ceiling.

"They have a light burnt out. I should tell someone," I mutter as I stare above our table.

I feel Charlotte's hand cover mine on the table. Swallowing thickly, I will my penis not to make a fool of himself under the table. I can feel him perking up and that's all I need—him standing at attention, slamming against the underside of the table, and making the glasses and plates clang together. And now I'm picturing my penis rising up like a phoenix and repeatedly smacking against the table like he's knocking on a door. Maybe that would impress her. *"Hey, Charlotte, look what my penis can do!"*

Charlotte's thumb starts tracing small circles on top of my hand, and I'm pretty sure the clanging of the table is about to commence in two seconds.

"Brooklyn is really pretty. A little crazy, but pretty. Does she make you happy?"

She makes me happy when she's passed out cold.

"Totally happy. She's great."

When she's not speaking. Or breathing.

"That's good. I'm glad you've found someone who makes you as happy as Rocco makes me."

Why can't Rocco just die already in a fiery crash?

"Are you guys ready to order or do you need a few minutes?" Our waitress interrupts as she stands next to the table with her pen and notepad.

Charlotte takes her hand off of mine and moves it into her

lap. I want her hand touching me again. It's such a casual thing for her to do, but it has me all tied up in knots. Now my penis has switched from a majestic, mythical bird to a fire-breathing dragon that wants to destroy the town. It's time for me to attempt the next item on the list, though, so I need to chill the fuck out.

"I'll have the Steak Diane and she'll have the Shrimp Scampi," I tell the waitress with a confident smile.

"I'm allergic to shellfish," Charlotte replies, giving me a funny look.

Shit! How could I forget that! Okay, be cool. Try again.

"I know, I was just making sure you remembered. Actually, she'll have the petite filet."

The waitress crosses it out and writes down the new order.

"I'm not really in the mood for steak," Charlotte states.

"Okaaaaay, she'll have the grilled chicken and avocado club."

Why is this so much cooler when guys do it in the movies?

"I don't like avocado. It's mushy and gross."

Son of a bitch!

At this point the waitress has crossed off and scribbled so much on the first page that she has to flip it over and start on a second page.

"Southwest chicken sandwich?"

Charlotte makes a face and shakes her head.

"Four cheese pasta?"

She shakes her head again and I start to panic. I already closed the menu and handed it to the waitress so I could look cool and smart. Now I look like a tool because I can't remember anything else on the menu. At this point it would probably be best if I could smack my penis into the table. It'd be more entertaining than this train wreck.

"What would you suggest?" I ask the waitress, trying to give her a look with my eyes that says "Help me the fuck out with this!"

"I would suggest you let her order for herself," the waitress replies in a bored voice.

She is so not getting a twenty percent tip.

"You can order anything on the menu!" I tell Charlotte with my best air of authority.

"Yeah, thanks. I was planning on doing that anyway. Are you okay?"

No! I'm not okay because I love you and you won't love me back if I don't even know what the fuck you want to eat!

"I'm great! Money is no object."

Now Charlotte and the waitress are both looking at me like I'm a douchebag, but I can't shut up.

"She'll have the most expensive thing on the menu."

"Seriously, I'm fine with just soup and salad," Charlotte states.

Soup and salad only costs ten dollars. That does not make me look cooler than Rocco.

"And she'll have a bottle of wine. I'll have a bottle too. As a matter of fact, buy those people a bottle of wine as well," I tell the waitress, pointing at two women sitting at the table next to us.

"You want to order wine for people you don't know?" the waitress asks.

Don't question me. The customer is always right, God dammit!

"We'll also have a cheesecake. A whole cheesecake. And so will those ladies over there."

"I'm pretty sure those ladies are already eating cheesecake," the waitress tells me.

Can you just help me the fuck out already?!

"Really, I don't need a whole bottle of wine. Or an entire cheesecake."

"We'll just have one of everything on the menu."

Take THAT, Rocco!

"I think I'll give you guys a few minutes," the waitress mumbles.

"No, no, it's fine. He'll have the Steak Diane, medium-well, I'll have the French onion soup with a side salad and Italian dressing, and we'll each have a glass of Moscato," Charlotte explains with a smile as she hands the waitress her own menu.

And just like that, the next item on the list dies a slow, painful, emasculating death.

Chapter 6

– Show Her Your Penis –

It's probably best if I take a few days off from the list. My mental state demands it. It's the last Friday of the month and that means Chicken Paprikash day. My mom makes the best Chicken Paprikash in the world and always invites a few people over when she makes it once a month. Tonight, my grandfather and his wife Sue are going to be joining us.

My grandfather George is pretty bad-ass. For the first few years of my life we lived with him, and I have some of the best memories ever from that time. He always let me watch whatever I wanted on TV, and I could swear as long as I never told my mom. My grandfather is the king of stringing together long, completely inappropriate words that hardly ever make sense but sound good coming out of his mouth when he's pissed off. He used to let me practice my run-on sentence curses until one day I said "Shit-poop-hell-freak-monkey" and I was banned from cursing. He shook his head at me sadly and told me he was disappointed in my lack of effort.

I haven't seen Pops in a few weeks, and since the entire freaking family is now aware of my love for Charlotte, I'm assuming he is too since my mom can't keep her mouth shut. Hopefully he'll be able to give me some good advice. He's been married twice; he's got to have *something* useful for me.

I walk into my parents' house without knocking and see my grandfather sitting on the couch watching the Game Show Network. What is it with old people watching game shows? When I'm old, please don't let me ever fall asleep in my recliner watching reruns of Family Feud.

"It's about time you got here. There's too much estrogen in this house," Pops complains as he lowers the volume on the TV.

"Where is everyone?" I ask.

"Sue's in the kitchen with your mother and Sophie."

"Dad's here, isn't he?"

"Like I said, too much estrogen," Pops deadpans.

Flopping down on the couch next to him, I let out a great big sigh.

When Pops doesn't say anything, I sigh again, hoping he'll get the hint.

"Just spit it out, kid. You know I don't do the whole touchy-feely thing, so don't expect me to ask you what's wrong."

I should be used to his crass bedside manner by now, but I'm not. Being subtle isn't one of his strong suits.

"So, there's this girl I'm in love with—"

"Yeah, Charlotte, I heard," he interrupts. "She's not out of your league, if that's what you're worried about."

Well thanks a lot. I wasn't thinking that at all until now.

"She doesn't know that I'm in love with her. We've known each other since birth, and it's a little hard to just come right out and tell her at this point," I explain.

"Stop being a pussy and just tell her," Pops replies.

"But what if she doesn't love me back?"

Pops shrugs and turns back to the TV. "Then grow a pair and get over it. Jesus mother of fuck Christ in a piss shithole, dick for brains, the answer is bathtub."

Well, this little talk sure helped to boost my confidence. As I get up from the couch to go in the kitchen and check on dinner, Pops grabs my arm and pulls me back down next to him.

"Sometimes I get a little nervous too. Here," he says, reaching into the pocket of his jeans and pulling out a bottle of pills. "Take one of these vitamins. They're good for brain stimulation and all that shit. Maybe they'll help you strap on a set and use that brain of yours to figure out a way to come clean with Charlotte."

Pops opens the lid and dumps two of the pills in my hand and then hands me his glass of water on the coffee table in front of him. Downing the pills in one swallow, I figure if they don't help stimulate my brain into coming up with a better idea for showing Charlotte I'm in love with her, maybe they'll calm my nerves about the ribbon cutting ceremony later tonight, or give me strong bones at the very least.

Something isn't right. Something isn't right at all. I want to have sex. I always want to have sex, but right now I want to have sex with the giant pair of scissors I'm currently holding in my hand and that wouldn't be good at all. Sex and scissors should never mix.

I could totally fit my penis into the finger holes, though.

I'm also contemplating having sex with the drainpipe attached to the building to my left. And maybe even sticking it to the Rhododendron bush to my right. I wonder if anyone would notice if I got down on my stomach and just started rubbing myself against the curb? Is it still illegal to have sex with trees in Ohio? I need to stick my penis in something right the fuck now.

I glance out at the crowd of people gathered in the parking lot of Minney's Adult Mart and wipe the sweat from my brow. Seduction and Snacks is the only distributor for Minney's, so this ribbon cutting ceremony is a pretty big deal. I don't have time for whatever is going on with me right now. I feel like I'm fifteen again and a gust of wind can get me hard.

"Dude, what's wrong with you. You look like you want to kill someone. Or rape the pair of scissors you're holding. Are you feeling okay?"

I glance at Tyler standing next to me and notice he's wearing corduroys. Those would feel really good right now if I rubbed my penis against them. All soft and rough at the same time. Like a ribbed condom, but better.

"Why are you looking at my legs like that? Stop it," Tyler scolds.

Shaking the dark thoughts from my head, I quickly turn away from him and try to think of something other than sex.

"I don't know what the fuck is wrong with me. I was fine at my parents' house but started feeling funny on the way over."

That woman has really pretty knees. I've never had sex with knees before.

"I hope that is a real fucking gun in your pocket and you're not excited to see me, otherwise this friendship is over. I don't swing that way," Tyler says in disgust as he stares at the crotch of my black dress pants.

Looking down, I realize I have the world's biggest hard-on tenting the front of my pants. I quickly turn away from the gathering crowd and un-tuck my dress shirt from my pants to try and cover it up.

"Oh my God, why won't it go down?!" I whisper yell.

"Try thinking about your mom naked. Wait, never mind, that just got me hard," Tyler says with a laugh.

"God dammit, shut up! Shit. Baseball, Pops taking a dump, puppies dying, Barney," I mutter, squeezing my eyes closed. "Holy fuck this is starting to hurt. Why won't it go away?"

"Wait, this is a serious problem? I thought you were just kidding," Tyler says after a few minutes of watching me mumble.

"It's a serious fucking problem! It feels like there's a penis inside of my penis trying to claw its way out and fuck everything in sight! I have to cut this ribbon in fifteen minutes. I can't stand in front of all of these people like this," I complain.

"Actually, this is probably the best place for you to be with this type of problem. I'm actually surprised there aren't people whipping it out in the parking lot. Try smacking it," Tyler suggests.

Before I can tell him that's a dumb idea, the palm of his hand smacks against my dick with the force of a two-by-four. I immediately bend over at the waist and start dry heaving and calling Tyler every name I can think of.

"Hey, Tyler! Is Gavin okay?"

Oh holy fuck, Charlotte is here!

I can hear her heels clicking on the sidewalk, bringing her closer and closer.

"Oh my God! She can't see me like this!" I panic, fumbling with the scissors and trying to get them to cover me.

"Hey, number five on the list is totally gonna happen right now!" Tyler says, clapping his hands together in glee.

"I'm not showing her my penis!" I whisper.

"Oh I'm pretty sure your penis has other ideas. He's like an angry armadillo trying to claw his way out of a bunker right now."

Staying hunched over, I turn around to face Charlotte, which is a really bad idea. Seeing Charlotte always turns me on. My face suddenly feels hot, and I'm lightheaded because all of the blood in my fucking body is now pumping through my penis. My angry armadillo penis.

"Are you okay? You don't look so good," Charlotte says as she puts her hand on my shoulder and starts rubbing small circles there.

"You might not want to touch him right now. That's probably going to make it worse," Tyler laughs.

"Shut the fuck up," I growl under my breath as I try to stand back and wince when I feel my penis shift against my boxer briefs.

"Do you have a stomach ache or something?" Charlotte asks.

"His ache is a little lower than his stomach," Tyler tells her with a smile.

"I have some Pepto in my car. I'll be right back," she tells me before turning away to rush back to her car.

"Mr. Ellis, we're about five minutes away from the ribbon cutting. The photographer is just finishing setting up his equipment," Chris Minney, the owner of Minney's Adult Mart, tells me as she walks up next to me.

Sucking up the pain in my groin, I stand up. Her eyes flash right down to my tented pants.

"Well, um, huh. It's good to see you're so excited about our grand opening. I think we have some things inside that will take care of that," she tells me with a pat on the back before walking away to talk to a few customers.

"Oh this is just awesome," I complain.

"How long have you had this problem?" Tyler asks.

Looking at my watch I'm shocked to realize just how long it's been.

"Almost two hours. I think my penis is broken. What if it

never goes down? I can't walk around like this forever."

"Well, you've still got five minutes. Go around back and spank one out," Tyler says.

"I'm afraid to touch it. What if it gets worse?"

"Dude, you don't have a gigantor penis. It can't possibly get any bigger. Maybe it's stress. I get stress hard-ons sometimes. If The Gap gets really busy and I don't have time to fold all of my jeans, it can turn into a problem."

Sometimes I wonder why we're even friends.

"Fuck. It's probably those stupid vitamins my grandpa gave me before dinner. I knew I shouldn't have taken those on an empty stomach," I complain.

"Pops gave you vitamins? That doesn't sound like something he would do. He's not that nice. What kind of vitamins were they?"

I shrug and try to shift my weight to my other leg to alleviate some of the pressure. My penis feels like it's going to explode. And not in a good way. In a blood and guts kind of way.

"I don't know. He *said* they were vitamins. They were little, blue things."

Tyler's eyes open wide and he bursts out laughing. "Oh fuck, dude, Pops gave you Viagra!"

I shake my head back and forth in denial. "What? No. There's no way he would just slip me Viagra and not tell me."

Right? RIGHT?!

"Oh he totally did. But don't worry, it's not a problem until your erection lasts for more than eight hours I've heard,"

Tyler says with another laugh.

"Okay, here's the Pepto. This should help," Charlotte says, coming back up to us and handing over the pink bottle while I scramble to hunch back over and dangle my arms in front of me.

"That's probably not going to help. But I bet taking him around back for about thirty seconds would," Tyler tells her.

"What?" Charlotte questions.

"Nothing. Just ignore him," I tell her, taking the bottle of Pepto and swigging some of it for her before handing it back.

"Oooh, look. The photographer is ready to take your picture, Gavin. Make sure both your heads are smiling," Tyler informs me before putting his arm around Charlotte's waist and moving a few feet away.

Chris Minney walks back over and puts her arm around my shoulders. "This is so much fun. I'm so glad you were able to make it out tonight and do the cutting for us."

The crowd gathers close as Chris turns us to face them and gives a little speech, thanking everyone for coming out to the grand opening.

As I move the scissors up to the red ribbon hanging in front of the walkway to the store, Chris pulls me closer and forces me to stand up straight. Right as I make the first cut and the flash of the photographer's camera goes off, the snipped ribbon falls, draping perfectly on top of my hard-on.

The caption under the picture in the paper two days later reads:

"Employee of Seduction and Snacks was VERY Excited to Cut the Ribbon for Minney's Adult Mart!"

Chapter 7

- Gag the Groin Ferret -

"Hold his calls for the rest of the afternoon, Ava!"

I look up from my desk to see Uncle Drew barging through my office door with Aunt Jenny right behind him.

"I don't answer his phone, Uncle Drew. Someone else does that," Ava tells him from the doorway.

"Aren't you his assistant?" Uncle Drew questions.

"Yeah, so?"

Uncle Drew rolls his eyes and ushers her out into the hallway before closing the door and locking it.

"What are you guys doing here?" I ask as Uncle Drew walks up to my desk and perches on the edge of it while Aunt Jenny takes a seat in one of the extra chairs.

"Well, I was originally coming here to commend you on an awesome boner shot in the paper the other day, but we have more pressing concerns to deal with right now. Jenny, tell him what he's won!"

Jenny looks at Drew in confusion. "Did he win something? I thought we were coming here to talk to him about sex?"

Oh my God.

"Gavin, I just found out from your mother that you've got a thing for Charlotte. What the fuck, dude? I can't believe you didn't come to me first. This cuts me deep, real deep, little man."

I groan as I rest my elbows on top of my desk and put my head in my hands. It was bad enough that number five on my list actually happened by accident the other day and that I had to jerk off six times in one night before my fucking hard-on would go away. Now I have to deal with this. Aunt Jenny and Uncle Drew consider themselves sex experts ever since they started giving "Spicing Up Your Sex Life" classes at the local community college. They've even been approached by a publisher to write a "How To" book, and all of this has gone to their heads. Their sex life is unconventional to say the least. It usually involves props that defy nature and almost always ends in someone going to the emergency room. Why anyone would want to take advice from them is beyond me. There was an incident when I was younger that involved Skittles. I don't know much about it, but I know that whenever my mom sees a bag of Skittles at the store, she dry heaves a little.

"I hear there's a list. Why haven't I seen this list? I should have had major input for this thing," Uncle Drew complains.

"Should I bring out the condoms and the banana now or do

you want to do that later?" Aunt Jenny asks him.

"Let's hold off on that, babe. First, I want to make sure this list he's using is in tip-top shape. Do you have 'tell her she has moist folds' on the list? That should definitely be on the list."

Drew reaches into the bag he brought with him and begins pulling out various items: a blender, a wheel of Vermont Cheddar cheese, and a jock strap are the first to land on my desk.

"Eeeew, that's ... no. No that is not on the list, nor will it ever be," I reply with a shudder.

"It should really be on the list Gavin," Aunt Jenny tells me seriously.

"What the hell does a blender and cheese have to do with my sex life?" I ask, picking up the wheel of cheese from my desk and turning it over in my hands.

Uncle Drew quickly grabs it from me and sets it back down. "All in good time, little asshole. Leave the cheese alone. It needs to stay at room temperature."

He continues pulling other items out of the bag that I really don't even want to know what they're going to be used for. Seriously? A small United States flag on a stick and a potted fern?

"Tell me you at least have something with role-playing on there?" Uncle Drew puts his hands on his hips and raises his eyebrows at me.

"I don't think that needs to be on the list. The last time we played with rolls you got a yeast infection in your eye," Aunt Jenny reminds him.

"Seriously? That can happen?" I ask Uncle Drew.

"You are never to speak of my yeast infection again," he warns me before turning around to look at Aunt Jenny. "And, honey, I'm not talking about that night with the tubes of Pillsbury dough. I'm talking about the Brady Bunch thing. Where I'm Greg and you're Marsha and you accidentally touch my penis at the dinner table while Alice serves us spaghetti."

I'm going to throw up. It's happening right now.

"Oh, I don't like that one. The blow-up doll we use as Alice looks at me funny. I think she's judging me," Aunt Jenny complains.

"Yeah, Alice is kind of a bitch. I'll blindfold her next time. Anyhoo, give me the list. I need to make sure you know what you're doing," Uncle Drew demands.

"Really, it's not necessary. I've got it under control."

Uncle Drew laughs and shakes his head at me. "You've puked in front of her, wrapped your schlong in a bow, and showed it to the entire city. You don't have it under control. What we have here is a failure to know what the fuck you're doing when it comes to chicks."

Getting up from my desk, he walks over to the dry erase board on my wall and uncaps a marker. He writes *moist folds* in big, black letters across the top.

"Oh my God, erase that," I complain.

"Fuck your mother, I'm not erasing it. This is important," Uncle Drew says before writing *role-playing* right underneath it.

"What temperature is your ball sack running at now?" he asks, turning around and narrowing his eyes at me.

"What? I don't know. Why are you asking me this?"

"Dude, to effectively produce sperm, your testicles need to be at least two degrees cooler than your core temperature. You should ice those little nuggets."

Is this really happening right now?

"Or he could just stick a pair of sunglasses on his little balls. That would be cute!" Aunt Jenny laughs and claps her hands together in glee.

"Ha-ha, totally! A little pair of Hello Kitty sunglasses and a bonnet for his un-fucking-cool testicles," Uncle Drew adds with a laugh.

"Can we please stop talking about my testicles?"

"You're such a buzz kill, dude. Okay, next. Gag the groin ferret," he states.

"I have no idea what that means," I complain, watching him write the words on the board.

"Um, hello? Whack off, gag the groin ferret, spank the monkey, bludgeoning the beefsteak, corralling the tadpoles, tweaking the toucan. You should be doing it at least eight to twelve times a day at this point."

I wince thinking about how I spent my evening after the ribbon cutting ceremony. I'm pretty sure I will never jerk off again.

"Can I bring out the condoms and banana now? Pretty please?" Aunt Jenny begs.

"I know how to put a condom on. There's no need for that," I tell her with a roll of my eyes.

"Are you sure about that? Last I heard, you were using them

as balloons," Uncle Drew says with a laugh.

"Oh my God, I was FOUR when that happened. It stopped being funny twenty years ago!" I complain.

"I just thought of another one, Drew. Make sure you do hallucinogenics before and after sex. You don't want your muscles tightening up on you," Aunt Jenny explains.

"Are you saying I should take drugs to have sex with Charlotte? I don't even understand what is going on right now."

Uncle Drew shakes his head at both of us before turning back to the board.

"She means calisthenics. Although a little pot might be just the ticket for you. If you get really stoned, it won't even matter that you have a small penis and have no idea how to please a woman," he says with a laugh.

"Fuck off, old man. I don't have a small penis. And I know how to please a woman," I fire back.

"Really? Quick, what are the ten erogenous zones on a woman? GO!" he shouts.

"I love when Drew touches my erroneous zones," Aunt Jenny says with a sigh.

Ignoring her, I run through every article I've ever read in a magazine or online. "GAAAAH! Fuck! Um, neck, lips, feet, inner thighs—"

"BZZZZZZZZZZ. WRONG, FUCKER!" Drew interrupts.

"What? Those were totally right. And I wasn't done yet," I argue.

"Those are wrong. Want to know what the ten erogenous

zones on a woman are? Number one: vagina. Number two: it doesn't fucking matter if you're touching her vagina right!" Uncle Drew shouts. "You are a disgrace. Your mother should have swallowed."

I give him the finger before he turns back to the board and begins scribbling furiously.

"Jenny, get the lawn darts and the graham crackers out of your bag. We're sending Gavin back to Sex-Ed. By the time we're done with you, Charlotte will be eating out of your hand. Literally. Jenny does this awesome thing with Nutella and a lint brush that will blow your mind."

Before my aunt and uncle walked into my office today, I had sworn off the list that Tyler and I made, vowing to never look at it again. Right now, that list is looking better and better.

Chapter 8

– Stick Your Tongue Down Her Throat –

The only way to forget everything I saw today is to bleach my eyes. But that really isn't an option since I'd still like to be able to look at Charlotte. Instead, I'm getting drunk.

"You know what word isn't used enough in the English language? Anal glands."

I nod in agreement, not even really paying attention to Tyler since I'm currently staring at Charlotte across the bar. She's so pretty and nice and pretty.

"I shouldn't have had that last shot of Crown. I can't feel my chalk," Tyler mumbles.

I haven't talked to Charlotte since Viagragate 2013 last week. She's been busy job hunting, and I've been busy being mortified. I knew she'd be here at this bar tonight because we've been coming to Fosters every Saturday night for as long as I can remember. My mom used to bartend here back when I was little, and the same couple still own the bar. Mr. and Mrs. Foster are in their seventies. They always let us drink for free and constantly ask us if we want to play P.O.R.N. I have no idea why they always ask that, and frankly, I don't want to know. Tyler swears that one of these times he's going to take them up on their offer because he thinks they'll take him into the backroom and show him their secret stash of old people porn.

All the alcohol I've consumed tonight hasn't erased my fear that I don't know how to please a woman. One sexual experience does not a master make. Ha! That rhymes with masturbate! Which I'm never doing again. What was I saying? Oh, yeah ... I know how to power up a Jack Rabbit and make a woman come three times within a minute, in theory. But what if I actually get the chance to be with Charlotte and I suck balls?

Not that I would suck balls. There shouldn't be any ball-sucking going on from my end of things.

Charlotte was already here at Fosters with a few of her girlfriends when we arrived an hour ago. I probably could have just gone over to her and pretended like she hadn't seen my giant erection the last time we were together, but instead, I waved to her and proceeded to act aloof, taking a seat on the opposite side of the bar.

I don't care if you saw me with a hard-on in public. It's totally cool. Happens all the time. I am totally secure with my penis pop-ups.

"I think I'm going to make a new list," I tell Tyler suddenly.

"I'm going to use some of your ideas and some of Uncle Drew's ideas and it's totally going to work."

I finish off my Jack and Coke and slam the empty glass on top of the bar.

"That's a good idea, bro. You should totally drive the Honda to the Californias," Tyler agrees.

"I just need to get rid of the disturbing things on Uncle Drew's list. Did you know that goat testicles dipped in honey are an aphrodisiac? Or maybe it's just honey ..."

Tyler suddenly smacks me on the arm. "Dude. Charlotte is totally staring at you. Wow, she's got a lot of facial hair."

I look across the bar and see a guy waving at us a few stools down from Charlotte.

"That's not Charlotte, you dick. That's Brad Manginallo. We went to school with him." I wave back at Brad and signal for him to come over and join us.

"Didn't we used to call him Mangina?" Tyler asks.

"Yes. And he threatened to kick your ass, so you might not want to do that again."

Brad comes over to us and I give him a pat on the back and pull out the stool on the other side of me.

"MANGINA!" Tyler yells in greeting.

"I see you haven't changed at all, Ty," Brad says with a laugh.

Brad was in a fraternity in college and a pretty cool guy, even if he was in the same frat as Rocco. For some reason, I was always told by my parents to stay far away from fraternities. It was actually one of their rules for letting me go away to college. No fraternities and no beer pong. Obviously, I obeyed the first rule. Not so much the second one.

"I hear you're some big wig at a dildo plant or something," Brad says with a laugh. "You always looked like the type of guy who liked to play with penises all day."

I take that back. Brad is not a cool guy anymore.

"Yeah, he makes all those toys your mom uses on her huge vagina," Tyler retorts. "MANGINA!"

Brad doesn't look happy about Tyler's repeated use of his nickname, and this makes me happy.

"Anyway, I'm working for my dad's financial company. I'm pulling in about two-hundred K a year," Brad tells us.

Was he this much of a douche in college?

"You're so awesome, Mangina," Tyler tells him with a smile.

"Don't you still work at The Gap and live in your mom's basement?" Brad asks him with another cocky laugh.

"Yeah, I still work at The Gap. But now I live in *your* mom's basement and pay my rent with daily sperm deposits on her face. MANGINA!"

Brad is really getting pissed off now, but it's obvious he's trying to keep his cool so he doesn't look like an asshole for punching Tyler in the face. Normally, I'm all for letting someone beat the shit out of Tyler when he's saying dicky things, but this is too entertaining to put a stop to.

"Either of you dicks know who that hot chick is on the other side of the bar? She's totally checking me out," Brad informs us.

I don't even bother looking across the bar because I'm pretty sure he's talking about Charlotte, and the idea that she would find him even remotely attractive is disgusting.

Eventually, I look over at her just to see if she's really eyeing Brad, but she's not. She's staring right at me. She smiles at me and I watch as she says something to one of her friends and hops down off of her stool on unsteady feet. She wobbles a little bit and her friends cheer and scream her name as she walks away from them and over in our direction. I'm pretty sure I heard one of them scream, "Give it to him, Charlie!" but I'm too busy wondering if I'm sober enough to punch Brad in the face if he says anything inappropriate to her.

My eyes grow wide and Brad immediately stops talking about how awesome he is as Charlotte squeezes her small body in between the two of us. With her back to Brad, she inches in between my legs and closer to me until our noses are almost touching.

"Hey, Gavin, why don't you introduce me to your friend," Brad says over Charlotte's shoulder.

I ignore him and stare directly into Charlotte's eyes.

"I'm a little drunk," she whispers.

"Me, too."

We smile at each other, and I can see Brad staring at us out of the corner of my eye.

She frowns. "I got into a fight with Rocco tonight."

"I'm sorry," I tell her, even though I'm not.

"My name's Brad. I work for McDonald Investments downtown. I'm sure you've heard of it."

I can feel Charlotte's warm breath against my lips as she continues to stare at me. She's never looked at me like this before, and I really hope I don't do something stupid.

"Don't lie, Mangina. You really work at the drive-thru of McDonald's flipping burgers. Do you want fries with that, Mangina?" Tyler says with a laugh.

"So, my girlfriends all dared me to do something to get back at Rocco. But I don't know if I should do it," she whispers.

I can't process what she's saying right now because she's moved in closer, and I can feel her breasts up against my chest. She's still a little wobbly on her feet, and since I'm such a gentleman, I place my hands on her hips so she doesn't fall.

"But I kind of have to do it since it's a dare, you know?"

I don't know. I don't know and I don't care about anything right now but keeping her exactly where she is and never letting her go. She fits perfectly in between my thighs and she smells amazing, just like always.

"We should all go outside so I can show you my new Porsche. It's parked right in front," Brad says loudly.

"No one cares, Mangina. Get in the kitchen and make me a Quarter Pounder!" Tyler tells him.

"I'm totally going to do this dare right now, okay? So don't freak out," Charlotte adds softly.

I nod in reply as I stare at her lips while they move. She has such pretty lips.

"Stop being a dick, Tyler," Brad threatens.

"At least I have a dick and not a MANGINA!" Tyler yells.

At this point, a few of the bar patrons have caught on to the shouting and join Tyler every time he yells Mangina. It's a fun word to yell, and I would totally be doing it if I wasn't so mesmerized by Charlotte's mouth.

Tyler and Brad are still arguing back and forth from either side of me, and before I can tell them to shut up, Charlotte suddenly leans forward and presses her lips to mine. I instinctively open my mouth on a surprised gasp and she takes the initiative, sliding her tongue past my lips and tangling it with mine. Her hands move to the back of my head, and she clutches the hair at the nape of my neck, pulling me harder against her mouth and deepening the kiss.

As half the bar starts chanting, "Mangina, Mangina, Mangina," I wrap my arms around her waist and hold her close, pouring everything I have into this kiss. Her friends dared her to kiss me so it means nothing to her, but it means everything to me and I want her to know that. All thoughts fly from my mind as our lips move together in perfect sync. She tastes like wine and I want to devour her. Her tongue glides against mine slowly, and I moan into her mouth, pulling her tighter against me. I move one of my hands up to her face, cupping her cheek as I deepen the kiss. I can't help myself; I slide my hand around to the back of her neck and grab a handful of her hair, clutching it in my hands. She whimpers against my lips and I'm instantly hard.

Charlotte suddenly ends the kiss and pulls her head back to stare at me. Her eyes are wide with shock, and I'm pretty sure she's completely mortified that she just kissed her best friend even if she's drunk. She probably thought it was a great idea at the time, and now she's regretting it because she can totally feel my hard-on pushing into her. A kiss between friends changes everything, even if it's just a dare.

She slides out from between my legs without saying a word, and I watch her walk back to the other side of the bar to her friends. They all start giving her high fives and scream her name in congratulations for a perfectly executed dare. They surround her, and in the midst of the chaos, she looks back over at me. She doesn't smile. She just stares.

Tyler smacks his hand against my back, and I break our eye contact to turn and look at him, hoping he witnessed what just happened so he can tell me it was real. It feels like a dream right now.

"Dude, that was the best thing I've ever seen," Tyler says in awe.

Thank God. He saw. It was real. I wasn't dreaming.

"Right? I'm freaking out a little bit right now. I can't believe that just happened."

Tyler nods his head in agreement and signals the bartender.

"We need two shots of Crown for me and my buddy here. The most epic thing in the entire world just happened and we need to celebrate," Tyler tells the bartender.

The guy pours us two overflowing shots of Crown, and when he walks away, we each grab our glasses and hold them up in the air.

"Tonight we toast to something amazing. A man was brought to his knees and will never be the same again," Tyler states.

I wasn't actually brought to my knees since I was sitting. But it works. If Charlotte had kissed me while I was standing, I probably would have lost all feeling in my legs.

We clink our shot glasses together, and as I bring mine up to my lips, Tyler adds, "To Mangina. Thanks for looking at some chick tonight and screaming 'WILD PUSSY!' at her. The punch she gave you to the face was the best thing I've seen in my entire life."

Rolling over in bed, I'm immediately assaulted with a pounding headache and the need to throw up. I groan as I move both of my hands up to my head and hold it in place. Slowly opening my eyes so that the bright morning sun doesn't make it feel like knives are stabbing through my skull, I scream and scramble up the bed until I slam against the headboard.

"HOLY FUCK WHY ARE YOU NAKED?!"

Tyler opens his eyes with a groan and glances up at me. "Will you stop shouting? It's too early for this shit."

I stare in horror as he reaches down and scratches his balls.

"Dude, WHY THE FUCK ARE YOU NAKED?" I yell again.

Tyler yawns and scoots up until his back is against the headboard next to me. I immediately move as far away from him as possible without falling off the edge of the bed.

He casually looks down at himself and then up at me. "Oh my God. I'm naked and you're afraid. It's the Ohio version of *Naked and Afraid.* You should be building a fire and trying to make a bikini out of palms right now."

"Why do we make such bad life choices?!" I shout.

"Naked … and afraid," he whispers menacingly with a laugh as he pulls one of legs up to rest his arm on top of it casually.

"What the hell happened last night? I don't remember anything after that last shot, except for a bunch of people screaming 'Wild Pussy' all night. Did that really happen?" I ask him as I get up out of bed and try to locate my cell phone.

"I roofied you because I wanted you naked … and afraid," Tyler says again in a sinister voice.

As I get down on my knees to look for my phone under the bed, I hear my front door open and close. Before I can yell at Tyler to put some fucking clothes on, my dad is in the bedroom doorway.

"Gavin, I brought over some of your mail that …"

He trails off when he sees me on my knees at the edge of the bed and Tyler casually lounging naked against the headboard.

"It's not what it looks like," I tell him with a sigh as he stares at both of us in horror.

"Yo, Mr. Ellis! Welcome to *Naked and Afraid,*" Tyler says with a wave to my dad.

"I feel like I'm in *The Crying Game* right now," Dad mutters with a sad shake of his head.

Tyler swings his legs over the side of the bed and stands up, putting his hands on his hips. "Did you bring your lovely wife with you this morning? I should go and say hi." Tyler smiles.

"Tyler, for the love of God, cover your junk. I just had breakfast and I might puke. Gavin, your mail is on the counter. And just so you know, your mother and I will still love you no matter what life choices you make."

Dad turns and walks away as Tyler swings around gives me a big smile. "Naked … and afraid, mother fucker!"

I don't know what happened last night, but at least I remember one thing. Charlotte kissed me. That means I have successfully completed one item on the list. I'm no longer oh-for-four. Game on, bitches!

Chapter 9

- The Telephone -

"So let me get this straight. There's a secret testing room at Seduction and Snacks and I haven't been invited? Remind me again why we're still friends?" Tyler asks as he kicks back in his chair and puts his feet up on my desk.

"It's not what you think. Women don't go in there and actually USE the toys. Get your feet off of my desk." I reach over and smack the bottom of one of his shoes.

"You're totally lying to me right now. I bet you have a two-way mirror in this place somewhere and you can just sit there watching hot chicks diddle themselves. I can't believe you've kept this from me all these years," Tyler complains.

I made the mistake of telling Tyler that we had a product-testing group coming in today to give us their thoughts about our newest toy, *The Telephone*. Every time we come out with something new, we send out free samples to fifty customers who've signed up to be on our testing list. They agree to use the product for at least a week and then come in on a scheduled date to discuss the product with other customers and fill out a survey about it. We do it in small groups of ten, and today the first group for *The Telephone* is showing up in a half hour. Tyler called me to see about meeting for lunch, and when I declined and gave him the reason, he hung up on me. Fifteen minutes later he showed up in my office.

"I'm not lying to you. It's actually pretty boring. We do have a two-way mirror, but I just sit on the other side taking notes about people's opinions."

Tyler shakes his head, still not believing me. "Liar. Take me to the diddlers."

Ava walks into my office and places the form I gave her an hour ago in front of me. "Gavin, I can't figure out the copier, so you're going to have to get someone else to make copies of these surveys."

"Ava, you're looking particularly slutty today. How about we get out of here and—"

"Stop talking to me," Ava interrupts.

Tyler places his hand over his heart and pretends to look wounded. "That hurts, Ava. Really hurts."

"Just being in the same room with you makes me want to start taking antibiotics," Ava complains before turning back to me. "So, anyway, I can't make these copies. It's too hard."

Sighing, I grab the survey and get up from my desk. "Ava, all you have to do is punch in the number of copies you want and then hit *print*. It's not that hard."

I don't know why I even bother; she's already on her cell phone, ignoring me.

"So, Ava, did you hear that our boy here sucked face with your sister Saturday night?" Tyler asks as she walks past him. She stops in her tracks and looks up from her cell phone.

"I may have heard something to that effect. What do you know?"

I watch as Tyler slides his feet off of my desk and leans closer to her. "I heard it was pretty hot. I was there, but I was otherwise occupied making fun of a man with a vagina. What did you hear?"

Ava shrugs and takes a step toward him. "I heard the same thing. I also heard that both parties were pretty into it and haven't spoken of said event since it happened."

Tyler nods and rubs his chin with his thumb and forefinger. "Interesting."

What is going on right now? These two can't be in the same room together without strangling each other, and now they're talking about me like I'm not standing right here.

"I think we should go somewhere and discuss this privately," Tyler informs her.

There is no way this can happen. I don't want Tyler divulging any of my secrets to Charlotte's sister. I'm sure I don't have to worry though; Ava hates him.

"I think that can be arranged," Ava replies.

Son of a bitch!

"Hello? I'm standing right here," I remind them.

They both turn around to look at me and then go right back to their discussion.

"I need to see a chick about a telephone. I'll meet you at Fosters in an hour," Tyler tells her.

"No one is meeting anyone in an hour. Ava, you don't get off of work until five."

Ava sighs and looks over her shoulder at me. "Gavin, I need to leave work early today for a doctor's appointment."

"DENIED!" I shout.

"I'll see you in an hour," Ava tells Tyler before walking out the door.

"She's a bitch, but she's got potential," Tyler muses as he stares at her ass while she leaves.

"You are not meeting up with her to tell her about the list," I demand as I head out the door to make copies of the survey. Tyler jumps up from his seat and follows behind me.

"I won't tell her about the list, vagina face. Give me a little credit here. She's got the inside scoop on Charlotte. I can feel her out, or up, and find out if that kiss the other night moved you up a few notches on Charlotte's love scale."

Sticking the survey into the copier, I slam the lid down and angrily punch the buttons for copies. "You can't even stand Ava. Why would you want to spend even a minute alone with her?"

Tyler shrugs and grabs the copies as they spit out of the machine. "I don't have to like someone to use them for sex. Seriously, it's like you've grown a vagina since the last time you banged a chick. How do you not know this information already?"

At this moment, I should probably threaten Tyler's life and tell him that Ava is like a sister to me and if he hurts her I will dismember him. But really it's Tyler I'm worried about. Ava is like a praying mantis on crack. She will not only chew off his head after she has sex with him, she will have sex with his headless body afterwards and then light it on fire.

I really don't want Tyler and Ava alone together where potential secrets could be leaked, but maybe Tyler can use his evil powers for good and find out what Charlotte is thinking.

We walk to the end of the hall and enter a room with a row of chairs facing the double-sided glass, and I take a seat in the middle. Tyler walks right up to the glass and puts his face against it.

"Holy hell, look at all those hot girls. And to think, right before they came here they probably had a few orgasms. Is this what Heaven is like?"

I roll my eyes at Tyler and check my watch. It looks like all ten consumers are in the room; we just need to wait for Aunt Liz to get here to start the meeting.

A few minutes later while Tyler is busy licking the glass, the door flies open and Aunt Liz comes rushing in, out of breath and looking frazzled. "Do you have the surveys?"

I hand them to her and she takes a moment to flip through them and catch her breath. "There was a breakdown on one of the machines in the plant and I've been on the phone with them for the past three hours trying to get it fixed. Of course it's the one producing *The Telephone* and everyone is freaking out."

Tyler turns away from the glass and walks up to Aunt Liz.

"You're a busy woman. How about you go back to your office and relax. I'll take care of this meeting."

She looks up from the surveys and raises her eyebrow at him. "You know that none of those women in there are going to actually masturbate today, right?"

Tyler crosses his arms in front of him and glares at her. "Why is everyone lying to me today?! It's like you WANT me to cry."

Aunt Liz sighs and turns back to me. "Alright, I think I'll head in there and see what's what. A few of them emailed me questions that I need to answer. Mostly they just want to know why we made a toy shaped like a phone and called it *The Telephone*."

"Why *did* you make a toy like that? It doesn't exactly shout, 'Hey, let's have sex!' unless it's designed for people who call hookers. Or maybe sex phone operators. I knew those chicks weren't faking it," Tyler complains.

"Actually, Gavin should know the story around *The Telephone*," Aunt Liz says with a laugh.

I look at her in confusion and shake my head. "No, I don't know any story. I just know my dad surprised Mom for their anniversary with the specs for the toy. Should I know the story?"

Aunt Liz crosses her arms in front of her and cocks her head to the side. "You seriously don't remember *telephone calls* when you were little?"

Wracking my brain to try and remember what the hell she's talking about, I have a faint memory of my parents constantly talking about making phone calls. I guess now that I think about it, they used to always put a movie on for me and tell me they had important phone calls to make. My mom was always really busy getting Seduction and Snacks up and running so I assumed she just had a lot of business calls to make.

"Oh my gosh, this is the best day ever," Aunt Liz states happily. "So, yeah, when they said they were making *phone calls* they were really having sex."

I can feel all of the coffee I drank this morning churning in my stomach. I know everyone's parents have sex. I'm not stupid. But MY parents shouldn't have sex. My parents should have only had sex to procreate, so twice. I'm going to vomit.

"Your dad really liked to make long distance phone calls. And pull his *antennae* out," Aunt Liz adds.

Covering my mouth with my hand, I shake my head back and forth.

"I'm pretty sure they made a phone call in your room while you were sleeping. Maybe even on your bed when you were gone. I bet they even made phone calls in the front seat of the car while you were oblivious in the back. You know, some *road calls* under the steering wheel."

Aunt Liz couldn't care less that I'm about to curl up in the corner, rocking back and forth.

"Claire is so awesome. I need to see if she'll add me to her friends and family plan," Tyler says. "It could be worse, Gavin. You think imagining about your parents having sex is bad, try thinking about your mom masturbating. Now THAT's disturbing."

Vomit in my mouth. VOMIT IN MY FUCKING MOUTH!

"Wait, that's not disturbing at all. Fuck, now I'm thinking

about Claire flicking the bean."

"Hooker, the group is waiting for you in there. What's taking so long?" my mom asks as she steps into the room and closes the door behind her.

"Oh, nothing much. Tyler was just talking to your son about you masturbating, and I was telling Gavin about *phone calls*. I think he needs a minute."

My mom looks at me with sympathy and mutters, "Oh dear. This could pose a problem."

"When I was twelve, we went to Disney World and you wouldn't let Sophie or me go in the jacuzzi tub in our room because you said dad's phone broke in the tub when he was making a phone call. Tell me he was really using his cell phone in the tub!"

Mom bites her lip and then winces. "If by cell phone you mean penis, then yes."

"OH MY GOD, MOM!"

She shrugs likes it's no big deal. "The maid hadn't stopped by yet. The jacuzzi was still contaminated."

I shiver in revulsion as I imagine what exactly the tub would have been contaminated with.

"Claire, I need to talk to you about getting on your cell phone plan. I'm going to need a lot of extra minutes," Tyler tells her with a wink.

"Do you kiss your mother with that mouth?" Aunt Liz asks.

"No. But I'll kiss Gavin's mother with this mouth."

Everyone needs to stop talking right now before my brain

explodes all over this fucking room.

"Speaking of kissing, Charlotte kissed Gavin the other night," Tyler adds.

"WHAT?!" Mom and Aunt Liz screech at the same time, whipping their heads in my direction.

"Oh my God, it's happening, it's really happening. We need to pick out a venue for the rehearsal dinner. Those things book fast," Mom states, pulling out her cell phone and clicking on Google.

"Jesus, Mom, it was just a kiss. Stop googling restaurants."

"Look up Stancato's, I love their salads," Aunt Liz says, standing behind my mom and looking over her shoulder.

"Fuck you, we're not doing the rehearsal dinner at Stancato's. Stop being such a whore for that place," Mom complains.

"Hello! Will you two cut it out?" I shout.

"I'm going to punch you right in the vagina if you don't pipe the fuck down," Aunt Liz argues with my mom.

How did I lose control of this situation so quickly?

"Ladies, could I interest you in a pool of Jell-O while you hash this out?" Tyler pipes up.

Perfect. Just perfect. I find out my parents never actually made any important phone calls when I was growing up and locked me in my room just so they could bang, and now my mom and my aunt are back to planning a wedding between Charlotte and me when I don't even know if she remembers that we kissed because she was so drunk.

This day can't possibly get any worse.

Chapter 10

- Make her Feel Sorry for You -

"Jesus, Dad, what the hell happened?" I ask in a panic as I rush into the hospital room to find him in a gown, hooked up to a bunch of machines.

Toward the end of the testing meeting, my mom got a frantic phone call from Uncle Drew letting us know that my dad was rushed to the emergency room because he thought he was having a heart attack. My mom immediately hightailed it out of there, leaving Aunt Liz and me to quickly wrap up the meeting.

"The dragon on the ceiling has bingo teeth," Dad says in a serious tone.

My eyebrows rise in surprise at his response, and I turn to my mom as she gets up from his bedside and walks over to me.

"Um, you should probably just ignore everything he says at

this point in time," she whispers.

"No, really. There are sharks on the planes in the window of the palm tree. My chin feels funny," Dad mutters, reaching his hand up and scratching his nose.

"What the fuck is wrong with him? Is he having a heart attack?" I question.

We both turn to look at him when he bursts out laughing, pointing at his feet. "There are kittens licking my toes! Look at the kittens! Hi, little kittens!"

Mom sighs and turns back to me. "The doctor is still running some tests, but right now it doesn't look like a heart attack or anything serious. He was at work and told Drew he felt funny— dizzy and nauseous. Then all of a sudden he told Drew he couldn't feel either of his arms so Drew freaked out and brought him here."

Dad continues to point and laugh at the kittens that aren't there, and a few minutes later, Tyler joins us in the room.

"I parked your car in the garage, Gavin. Saw Drew and Liz outside. They're going to call everyone and let them know what's going on."

Tyler tosses my car keys to me and I put them in my pocket. I was so worried when we got here that I jumped out of my car in front of the emergency room and told Tyler to go park my car.

"So what's going on with big daddy? Is he dying?" Tyler asks as he sidles up to my mom and puts his arm around her shoulder.

She elbows him in the ribs and moves away. "I'm going to chop off your arm and beat you with the bloody stump. Gavin,

I'm going to go get some coffee. Keep an eye on your dad. Call me on my cell if he starts crying again."

Mom walks over to my dad and kisses him on the cheek before leaving the room. I move around to the side of his bed and take the seat my mom had been occupying.

"How are you feeling, Dad?" I ask.

"These chicken feet have pot whistles," my dad complains to the ceiling.

I sigh and look over at Tyler. He looks a little guilty. He's biting his nails and staring wide-eyed at my dad.

"Don't worry, I'm sure all of your wishes that he would die so you could make a move on my mom aren't coming true," I tell him with a laugh, trying to lighten the situation now that I know Dad isn't really having a heart attack.

"My penis is a pirate and I fight crime with a meat whistle sword. Who wants to pet my goat?" Dad asks.

"Oh, Jesus, you're going to kill me," Tyler moans.

"What are you talking about?"

Tyler stops biting his nails and begins pacing back and forth at the end of the bed.

"I need to tell you something, but you have to promise not to kill me," Tyler begs.

"Dad, I'll be right back," I tell him as I get up from my chair and move around to the end of the bed, grabbing Tyler's arm to get him to stop pacing.

"FAIRYDUST!! EVERYONE GETS FAIRYDUST!" Dad yells.

"Oh my God, this is bad. This is really bad," Tyler mutters as he stares at my dad.

"Tyler, what the hell is your problem?"

He sighs and turns away from my dad to look at me nervously, biting his lip. "So, remember yesterday morning, *naked and afraid?*"

"I thought we agreed to never speak of that again," I complain.

"Yeah, well, I just now remembered why I was naked. The night before, after you passed out, I made some chocolate candies in your kitchen. And then ate one."

I stare at him in confusion and then shrug my shoulders. "Yeah, and?"

Tyler bites his lip again and glances nervously between my dad and I.

"Shhhhhh, the puppies are making glue," Dad warns us.

"And, um, well, they were 'shroom chocolates."

He looks at me worriedly and I'm still not catching on so I shrug again.

"Hence the reason for my nakedness. I was high that night," Tyler adds.

Still not getting it, I stare at him in confusion.

"I made six chocolates and I ate one. But when I left your house that morning, there were only four chocolates left. Which means ..."

I turn my face away from Tyler slowly and stare at my dad who now has his leg bent and his foot in his hand, staring at it intently.

"There's no marshmallow in this. WHY THE FUCK ISN'T THERE ANY MARSHMALLOW? Tell the beaver to stop singing. I don't like that song."

Oh no. Oh my God. My dad stopped over that morning to drop off my mail.

"So yeah. I'm guessing this means your dad is tripping his balls off," Tyler mumbles. "Hey, at least it's not a heart attack."

Now that I have this information, I should be a little bit relieved. I mean, Tyler's right. At least it's not something serious. But now I have to tell someone, like my mother. And she is going to kick my ass. I could just take this information to the grave, but I can't let the doctors continue to test him for no reason. That's just cruel.

"Gavin, oh my God, I got here as soon as I heard. Is your dad okay? What's going on?"

Turning, I see Charlotte rush into the room and she throws herself in my arms. It feels so good to have her body pressed up against mine that for a minute I forget about the problem at hand. She squeezes me tightly to her, and I take a moment to just breathe her in. We haven't spoke at all since the kiss, which is really unusual for us. We talk every single day whether it's in person or via text. I'm not embarrassed at all by what happened between us at Fosters, but the fact that I haven't heard from her since then makes me wonder if *she* is. And if she is, at least she's able to put it aside and be here for me. At least the fact that she still cares about me hasn't changed. But if I tell her that my dad isn't really sick, and the reason for him being in the hospital, she's probably going to be pissed and no longer concerned for my well-being.

I know I'm an ass. Don't judge me.

Staring over her shoulder at Tyler, I give him a look that says "I really want to kick your ass right now, but I won't because I'm an awful person and I'm going to use this to my advantage."

"They think he might be having a heart attack. I'm so worried," I tell her, burying my face in the side of her neck and holding her tighter.

"I HAVE A MEAT WHISTLE!" my dad yells.

Charlotte pulls away from me and looks over at him.

"Did he just yell about his meat whistle?" she whispers.

"Um, yeah, just ignore him. It's the drugs they have him on to keep him comfortable," I tell her quickly.

Tyler laughs behind us and I shoot him an angry glare.

"Alright, I just spoke to the doctor down in the cafeteria and it looks like there's nothing—"

"MOM! Thank God you're back," I interrupt her quickly.

Stepping away from Charlotte, I pull mom over to the door and lower my voice.

"So, here's the thing. Dad accidentally ate a 'shroom chocolate that Tyler made at my place the other night so he's not having a heart attack. He's just really, really high. But Charlotte doesn't know that and she's worried about me, so we're just going to go with it, okay?"

I stop rambling and try not to wince at the wide-eyed look my mom is giving me. The look that says her head is about to explode.

"You have got to be fucking kidding me," she finally mutters. She leans around me and stares angrily at Tyler. Tyler just shrugs and waves at her while Charlotte steps over to the side of my dad's bed and grabs his hand.

"It's going to be okay, Uncle Carter. You just concentrate on getting better and I'll make sure Gavin is okay," she tells him softly.

I smile brightly at Charlotte's words but quickly wipe the happiness off of my face when I turn back to see my mom glaring at me.

"Charlotte, have you made any phone calls with Gavin yet? You're probably going to need to help him pull out his antenna, I don't think he knows how it works," Dad explains.

Mom laughs, patting me on the back when she sees the look of horror on my face before walking around me to go over to my dad. Charlotte moves out of her way and comes back over to me.

"Wow, I can't believe how out of it your dad is. I feel so bad. Are you having a problem with your phone? Do you need me to take a look at it?" she asks.

"Gavin, pull out your phone and show her how broken it is," Tyler says with a laugh.

"There's nothing wrong with my phone. It works perfectly fine," I growl.

Charlotte holds her hand out in front of me. "Don't be stubborn. Put your phone in my hand. I'm really good with phones."

Tyler laughs again and I reach over and smack him in the arm.

"Really, my phone isn't broken," I reiterate.

"Dude, Charlotte is *really* good with phones. Let her touch it," Tyler snorts.

"Gavin, if you don't give me your phone right now, I'm going to reach into your pocket and take it out myself," Charlotte argues.

"I am so turned on right now," Tyler whispers.

"I have a better idea. Why don't we get out of here for a little while and give my mom and dad some peace and quiet," I tell her, trying to change the subject.

Charlotte sighs and looks back over her shoulder at my parents. "That's probably a good idea. Your dad needs his rest and you need to do something to take your mind off of what's going on with him."

Elated by the idea that I'm going to spend some more quality time with Charlotte, I tell my parents goodbye and leave Tyler with them. He deserves the punishment of my mother's wrath for the rest of the afternoon after what he did.

Charlotte grabs my hand as we head toward the door, and I try not to skip across the room in happiness when she laces her fingers with mine.

"We can do whatever you want today. It's your choice. But just so you know, I *will* have my hand on your phone by the end of the night," Charlotte threatens.

"MAKE SURE HE PUTS A PROTECTIVE COVER ON HIS PHONE!" my dad screams at us as we exit into the hallway.

Chapter 11

- Show Her Your Nuts -

"So hypothetically, what would you say if I told you I broke up with Rocco?" Charlotte asks.

We've been at my apartment ever since we left the hospital and we've consumed quite a bit of beer. All of our empties clang together as Charlotte leans forward and slams her bottle on the coffee table before curling her legs underneath her, sitting next to me on the couch.

For most of the afternoon, we watched mindless TV and didn't talk about anything important. It seemed like we were both trying to avoid the white elephant in the room. But now that we have some alcohol in our system, more important issues are being discussed.

"You broke up with Rocco?" I ask in shock, trying my hardest to keep the elation from my face.

"I said hypothetically," she reiterates.

Dammit all to fucking hell.

How do I answer this? How does she want me to answer this?

"Um, Rocco is a really nice guy."

BULLSHIT!

Charlotte sighs heavily and turns to face me on the couch. "That's not what I asked. I know Rocco is a nice guy. One of the best. I want to know how you would feel if I wasn't with him anymore."

Feelings? Fuck, she wants to talk about feelings? I feel like I want to go streaking through the streets if she's no longer with Rocco. I'm guessing that's not what she's looking for here, though.

I need to talk to my dad. This is really sad that I'm a grown man and need my dad, but I do. Fucking Tyler and his 'shroom chocolates. If I call my dad now, he'll probably just tell me to eat the butter because the cornflakes are watching.

"Can you hold that thought for a minute? I just realized I forgot to send an email out for work. It's really important," I add when I see the disappointed look on her face.

"Fine, but hurry up. I'm feeling a little buzzed and I want to talk."

Standing up and walking backwards toward the doorway, I watch as she pulls her legs out from underneath her and leans forward to grab her beer bottle. The front of her shirt falls open and I have a perfect view of her red, lace-covered breasts.

Sweet Jesus. What was I doing? What day is it? Did I eat a 'shroom chocolate by mistake?

"Stop staring at my boobs and hurry up," she tells me with a smirk.

I flinch and look up into her eyes, a little shocked that she hasn't made any attempt to lean back so I can't see down her shirt anymore. It's like she WANTS me to keep staring at her boobs. I feel like it's my civic duty to continue staring at her boobs. Even *they* want me to keep staring, the way they're all pushed up in her bra and looking so amazing without even trying. I think one just winked at me. Do boobs wink? Does beer contain eleventy-seven thousand percent alcohol by volume now?

Remembering my purpose for suddenly getting up from my spot next to her, I start backing up again, my eyes never leaving her winking boobs.

Eventually, I have to pull my gaze away as I round the corner of the living room and into the kitchen. Turning around, I race across the room and wedge myself between the fridge and the cupboards, pulling my cell out of my back pocket and dialing the first number I can think of.

As the phone rings, I peek my head out from around the fridge to make sure Charlotte didn't follow me in here.

"This better be good. I have a naked woman on the roof and a jar of almonds toasting in the microwave," Uncle Drew answers.

"Charlotte wants to talk about feelings!" I whisper yell into the phone.

"Carrots want to dog above ceilings? Dude, are you stoned?" Uncle Drew replies.

Taking a quick glance around the fridge again, I raise my voice a little louder, cupping my hand around my mouth to contain my words.

"Charlotte is in my living room. I just saw her boobs. I repeat, I JUST SAW HER BOOBS!"

There's silence on the other end of the line and I wonder if the call dropped.

"Uncle Drew?" I whisper.

"I'm here, I'm here. Fuck! I wasn't expecting this phone call for at least another seven to ten days. Aunt Jenny hasn't finished making the bar graph, and we still have statistics to process. Shit! Okay, don't panic. Did you TOUCH the boobs yet?" Uncle Drew questions.

"No! But she wants me to tell her how I feel. What the fuck do I do?"

Uncle Drew sighs. "Fuck. Feelings. Damn, she's bringing out the big guns. Okay, here's what you do. You distract her. Chicks are like squirrels on crack. Throw a nut in their direction and they'll forget what they just wanted five seconds before," Uncle Drew explains.

"So, you're saying I should just change the subject when she asks me how I feel?"

"Fuck no! I'm saying, if she asks you some girly shit, you throw your nuts at her. Whip those puppies out, roll them around in your hands, and get her to focus on those bad boys instead."

Remind me again why I thought calling him was a good idea?

"I'm not showing her my balls!" I whisper angrily into the phone.

Uncle Drew laughs and before he can give me any other stellar advice, I hear Aunt Jenny in the background.

"Drew, did you just tell Gavin to show Charlotte his balls to avoid talking about how he feels?"

"Babe, why did you get down from the roof? The almonds are almost ready and the pickled relish is cooling on the stove," Uncle Drew pleads.

"Drew Parritt, are you telling Gavin not to talk about his feelings?" Aunt Jenny demands again.

I hear a rustle of fabric over the line and then Uncle Drew shouts, " Jenny, look at my nuts!"

Peering around the corner, I see Charlotte walk into the room and look at me questioningly.

"Ooooh, I love your nuts. Don't forget to grab the salad thongs. I'll see you on the roof."

A few seconds later, Uncle Drew comes back on the line as Charlotte walks right up to me and stands a few inches away, staring into my eyes.

"What did I tell you? Nut tossing works every time. Good luck. I gotta go. There's a few orgasms calling my name."

The dial tone sounds in my ear and I end the call, slowly lowering my arm down and placing my phone on the counter next to me, my eyes never leaving Charlotte's.

"Are you done with work stuff?" she asks.

I nod my head in response, unable to speak because of her close proximity. I want to touch her boobs. They're right in front of me, straining against the front of her T-shirt. They're doing this on purpose! They know I can't just reach out and touch them whenever I want. Fucking boob teasers.

"We kissed the other night," Charlotte whispers.

I swallow thickly and nod again, trying not to look directly at the boobs since it would be rude.

"What were you feeling right when we kissed?" Charlotte asks, leaning in closer so that her boobs are now pressed up against my chest.

I want to snuggle her boobs and I want to kiss her and never stop, and she wants feelings! I have feelings, dammit! I have all the feels! But what if my feels aren't the same as her feels and I look like an idiot because of my feels? I don't want to look like an idiot!

Staring down the front of her shirt, her warm breath on my face, I reach for the fly of my jeans without even thinking about what I'm doing.

"I HAVE NUTS!"

Chapter 12

Here's to You, Mrs. Robinson...er, Ellis

"You look guilty. Why do you look guilty?" Tyler asks as soon as he hops into the passenger seat of my car and I take off.

How the fuck does he do that? Of course I feel guilty. My best friend stuck her hand down my pants last night and jerked me off. And when I tried to reciprocate and wound up ripping her underwear by accident, she left without saying a word. I'm way beyond feeling guilty. I'm fucking mortified.

My mom had a meeting she couldn't miss this morning and my dad is being released from the hospital. She didn't ask so much as tell me I would be picking him up today.

"You need to pick your dad up from the hospital. And take him wherever he wants to go. I don't care if he has to go back to the doctor for an enema, you will go with him and hold his hand."

Even though Tyler spent half the evening with my parents last night after I left the hospital with Charlotte, I didn't feel like that punishment was enough for him, considering he roofied my dad, so I told him he was coming with me.

"I have no idea what you're talking about. I don't feel guilty," I finally reply, refusing to look in his direction.

"Liar, liar, you're a fucking whore. Spill it," Tyler demands as I stop at a red light.

I can feel Tyler's eyes boring into me from the other side of the car, and I know my face is heating up and turning red.

"Oh my fuck. Is that a hickey on your neck?" Tyler shouts.

Craning my neck, I look into the rearview mirror, and sure enough there is a little red mark right below my ear. Hot damn.

"I think you have your answer right there, bro. When a chick gives you a hickey, she means business."

Looking away from the mirror, I glance over at him in confusion. "What are you talking about?"

Tyler shakes his head at me. "Dude. She marked you. Now, every chick that sees you is going to know you're taken. She should have just pissed all over you and been done with it. Golden shower, party of one!"

I'm sure that's not why Charlotte did it. It was the heat of the moment and all that shit. Tyler's insane.

"So, you made a move. Little Gavin is all grown up. It brings a tear to my eye. Under the shirt AND under the bra? Did you blow your load in your pants as soon as you touched her tits? Is that why you feel guilty?"

I scoff at him and roll my eyes. "What are we, twelve? Did you seriously just ask me that?"

I know, I know. I totally DID blow my load like ten seconds after she touched me, but I'm not about to tell Tyler that.

"Hey, it happens to the best of us. I once came in my pants when I was thirteen and Christy Collins made me play with her My Little Ponies."

I laugh and glance Tyler's way as I wait for a red light to change. "Was Christy Collins THAT hot when she was thirteen?"

Tyler shakes his head and pulls his cell phone out of his back pocket. "It had nothing to do with her. Have you ever played with My Little Ponies? They have such silky smooth hair and cute little butts. Twilight Sparkle is my favorite."

I can't form words right now, even if my life depended on it.

"Dude, did you jerk off to a My Little Pony?" I ask in disgust.

"See? I knew you'd judge me. It's not like that at all. It's all about her personality," Tyler argues.

"It's a fucking plastic horse! Holy shit, you don't bang animals do you?" I yell in horror.

"Oh my God, that's just sick, Gavin. Really, I expected better from you. Can we please change the subject? I really don't like discussing my Bronie status with someone who doesn't live the lifestyle," Tyler complains.

"Did you just say Bronie? What the fuck is that? Is this some sort of club or something?"

"Not that you care, but yes. Bronies are a select group of men who appreciate the beauty and personalities of My Little Ponies,"

Tyler explains.

"And by *appreciate* I'm assuming you mean *jerk off to*," I say with a laugh.

"IT'S NOT LIKE THAT!"

I just nod, trying to contain my laughter and overall disgust from this conversation.

"So, did you close the deal and fuck Charlotte?" Tyler asks, changing the subject.

"Stop. I would never fuck Charlotte. I would make love to her gently," I tell him.

"Alright there, McSensitive Pansy Ass. Did you make sweet, sweet love to your beautiful goddess?" Tyler asks, folding his hands under his chin and batting his eye lashes at me.

"No, we didn't get that far. I did rip her thong, though," I tell him sheepishly.

"BOOM! That JUST happened! Maybe you really do have a penis hiding between your legs after all."

Before I can call Tyler a My Little Pony-fucking freak, he puts his phone up to his mouth and speaks into it.

"Siri, where is the closest Victoria's Secret?"

"I do not understand the question, Hot Lover Boy Big Penis Man Titty Tickler."

Listening to Siri spout off the name Tyler makes her call him, I roll my eyes and shake my head.

"Don't judge me. Siri speaks the truth," Tyler says distractedly as he presses the speaker button and talks into his phone once again. "Siri, my friend needs to buy some thongs for a chick he almost banged. Where the fuck is Victoria's Secret?"

"I do not appreciate your tone of voice, Hot Lover Boy Big Penis Man Titty Tickler."

Tyler curses at his phone.

"Why exactly do we need to go to Victoria's Secret for thongs?" I question.

"Um, hello? Item number seven on the list. Buy that bitch some lingerie."

Damn, I forgot about that one. Come to think of it, I'm surprised I even know my name after what happened last night with Charlotte. I don't even need to close my eyes to remember what it felt like to have her small, warm hand wrapped around me. Things escalated quickly between us in my kitchen, and I hope to God she doesn't have any regrets because I want a repeat performance as soon as possible. One where I actually last more than a few seconds. I have no idea what any of this means. Is she going to break up with Rocco now? Was last night a fluke because she was a little buzzed and it will never happen again? Why the fuck can't vaginas come with instruction manuals?

"Siri, you are a worthless piece of shit," Tyler complains.

"I could say the same about you."

"You fucking whore! Take a note, Siri. Go fuck your mother."

"This note has been recorded and added to your Notepad."

"FUCK YOU!"

"I do not understand your request, but I could search the web for 'fuck you.'"

"How about you search the web for why you're such a

cunt cake?"

"I don't think you appreciate me anymore, Hot Lover Boy Big Penis Man Titty Tickler."

"I'm sorry, Siri. I still love you."

"Impossible."

"PIPE THE FUCK DOWN AND TAKE A COMPLIMENT, YOU WHORE FACE BAG OF DICKS!"

Tyler tosses his cell in the center console and crosses his arms angrily in front of him.

"You seriously need a girlfriend. The relationship you have with Siri is disturbing," I tell him as we pull into the hospital parking lot.

"She's a bitch, but she's the only woman who understands me. And anyway, do you know any single women who would call me Hot Lover Boy Big Penis Man Titty Tickler?" he questions.

"I don't know any single women who could even just think that in their heads without throwing up in their mouths a little," I reply as I find a parking spot.

"Exactly. So, anyway, I'm going to guess your mom never told your dad about the whole 'shroom chocolate incident since I haven't heard about any hits out on me."

"You're lucky my dad never found out. Your body would be buried in a ditch somewhere."

"Aww, I think Carter would take it easy on me. That's the best trip he's ever had. You're mom probably got laid in the hospital," Tyler says with a frustrated groan. "I knew I should have stuck around longer. She probably would have thrown me a bone."

"In what universe would my mother ever throw you a bone?"

"In Tylerverse. Where there are rivers of beer and naked chicks servicing me all over the land," Tyler replies.

"I'm going upstairs to take a nap. I still don't feel all that great," my dad tells us as we walk into my parents' house an hour later.

"I could make you a snack if you'd like. Maybe some delicious chocolates?" Tyler shouts to his retreating back as my dad makes his way up the stairs. I shoot him a dirty look as the front door opens behind us and my mother walks in carrying an armload of paperwork.

"How's your father?" she asks, handing me the paperwork so I can set it on the foyer table.

"He's okay. He just went upstairs to lie down."

Tyler walks up next to me and winks at my mom.

"Hello, Claire. You're looking beautiful as always," Tyler says with a cocky smile.

My mom, who normally looks like she wants to chop off Tyler's balls and feed them to the nearest shark tank, gets a sudden gleam in her eye. This is not good.

"Hey there, hot stuff. How about you come over here and show Mama a little sugar," my mom says with a sultry purr to her voice that I've never heard before. It makes me wince and gag a little.

"Um, I don't ... what?" Tyler squeaks.

My mom saunters over to Tyler with a sway of her hips and stops right in front of him, letting her tongue skim her bottom lip.

I'm going to puke. I'm totally going to puke all over the floor right now. What the fuck is she doing?

Mom presses her palm against Tyler's chest and leans in close until her lips are grazing his ear. "You're heart is beating so fast, big boy. Want Mama to make it all better?"

Tyler's face immediately turns ten shades of red, and his eyes are so wide I'm surprised they haven't popped out of his head. His fantasy has come to life and he's realizing it's really a nightmare.

"What's wrong, Tyler-pooh? I thought this is what you wanted?"

Tyler shakes his head back and forth frantically, looking over at me in a panic. As disgusting as this is to witness right now, I'm pretty sure Tyler is going to be scared straight when it comes to my mother and his sexual comments.

Mom drapes her arm around Tyler's shoulder and smiles at him. "Don't be afraid. I'll be gentle with you. I'll make sure to use the small strap-on."

She runs her finger down Tyler's cheek, and I'm pretty sure if I look close enough I'll see that he's wet himself. I'm suddenly cured of my nausea and totally on board with whatever warped plan Mom has brewing in her head right now.

"Um, I think there's been a mistake," Tyler stutters as he looks back and forth nervously between my mother and me. I just shrug at him and slide my hands in my pockets. He's not getting any help from me. I'm actually kind of proud of Mom right now. She is one hundred percent committed to this performance and will do whatever it takes to make Tyler back off, including scarring him for life.

"Come on, baby. Mama wants you to take it like a good boy," she coos.

"What?! No! That's okay. I don't need Mama to give me anything. Seriously, stop saying that!" Tyler says in a rush.

"Gavin, you should go and give us some time alone."

"NO! DON'T YOU DARE LEAVE ME!" Tyler shouts, reaching his hands out to me.

Moving out of his reach, I walk toward the door with a laugh as my mom wraps both of her arms around Tyler and squeezes him tight. "Sorry, dude. This is something I definitely don't want to see."

As I open the door and step out onto the front porch, I've forgotten all about my disastrous evening with Charlotte, thanks to my mom. Maybe it's time to scrap the list and just tell her how I feel.

I look back over my shoulder as the door closes behind me, and it's like something out of a horror movie. Tyler is screaming and flailing his arms all around and my mom reaches around from behind him, smacks her hand over his mouth, and pulls him back away from the door right before it closes.

Charlotte

Chapter 13

~ Spiderman ~

"It was a disaster, Rocco. A total disaster," I complain with a sigh.

"I'm confused. How was it a disaster when you touched his penis?"

I glare at Rocco and signal the bartender for a refill of my Moscato. This is going to take a lot of booze.

"I think I'm going to need you to start at the beginning because I really don't understand what the problem is. You've been following the list we made and things are moving along quite well, if I do say so myself," Rocco replies, giving himself a pat on the back.

I've done something stupid. Something really, really stupid and now that it's done, I can't take it back. And no, I'm not talking about shoving my hand down Gavin's pants last night. That wasn't stupid, that was genius. Contrary to popular belief, I've never touched a penis before. Wait, that sounds bad. That sounds like everyone thinks I go around touching penises. No one thinks I'm a slut. At least I hope they don't. But I'm pretty sure they think I gave up the goods to some idiot in high school that was in Gavin's band. Let me set the record straight here–I didn't. I just kind of sort of made people think that. And by people, I mean Gavin. I know, I know. I should be hanging my head in shame, but what the fuck was I supposed to do? Nothing else was working. I tried going out with a few guys, I tried kissing a few guys … nothing got a reaction out of him. And telling a teensy, tiny, little white lie about losing my virginity only made him go straight into the arms of that whore, Shelly Collins. He took her to prom! It should have been me, God dammit!

Shit, I'm getting off track here. I should probably do what Rocco says and start at the beginning. But the beginning was a really long time ago. I don't even remember when I actually fell in love with Gavin. It feels like forever. The problem is that we grew up together and our parents are best friends. Our families have always done everything together, and I'm like a little sister to him. I'm sure he still looks at me and sees a girl in pigtails that used to suck her thumb. That is NOT a turn-on. Wait, actually I think it is. I'm pretty sure they have porn for that. And if I'm not mistaken, Rocco even put it on our list that I should dress up as a schoolgirl for Gavin. Fuck. I probably should have started with that instead of the easy stuff like making him jealous and forcing him to look at my cleavage.

So, let's go back to the middle instead of the beginning. I met

Rocco a few months ago at a sorority mixer, and he very quickly became one of my best friends. Obviously, he didn't understand why I turned down every single guy who asked me out, so I had to come clean with him. I had to tell him that I've been in love with my best friend practically since birth. One night over Pink Poodle martinis, Rocco started to make a list on a scrap of paper from my purse of things I could do to get Gavin to notice me. One thing turned into twelve, and now here I am with a fake gay boyfriend, a few drunken kisses, and one sloppy hand job.

Gavin probably thinks I'm a drunken idiot. I've kissed him twice now after copious amounts of alcohol, and last night, I took the bull by the horns. Or the penis by the base.

"Rocco, I can't rehash what happened last night. It's too mortifying."

Rocco puts his arm around my shoulder and pulls me close, giving me a squeeze. "I know, sweetie. But I haven't gotten laid in months, and I need to live vicariously through you. Tell me everything."

The bartender sets down another glass of wine in front of me, and I grab it, taking a huge gulp before beginning.

"So, you know that I went to Gavin's place last night so he could get his mind off of his dad being in the hospital. And of course, since I had a few beers, I had the courage to actually ask him about that kiss last week," I start. "As soon as I asked him, he got up from the couch and said he had to do something really important for work."

"Let me stop you right there. What was Gavin wearing?"

Rocco asks.

I scowl at him and smack his arm. "Cut it out. It's bad enough that you drool over him every time you see him. What he was wearing doesn't matter."

To be honest, though, I really can't blame Rocco for drooling over Gavin. He is definitely drool-worthy. Gavin is six feet tall and the hottest guy I've ever seen. I don't even know when it happened—when he turned from annoying little boy to hot as fuck. It's almost like he went to sleep one night as a little kid and woke up a man—a man with a great body and a gorgeous face with a dimple in each cheek that is to die for. He has short brown hair, chocolate brown eyes, and sometimes if I'm lucky, day old stubble that I want to lick.

Rocco shakes his head sadly at me. "It ALWAYS matters, Charlotte. I need to get the visual correct if I'm going to help you. Was his T-shirt molded to his well-defined chest? Did his jeans hug his scrumptious ass? Was he wearing that cologne that smells like a crisp fall day?"

Rubbing my fingers against my temples and closing my eyes, I ignore Rocco's stupid questions. Why the hell did I think it would be a good idea to enlist my gay friend to help me out with this?

"If you want me to tell you what happened, shut up. This is serious. I touched a penis for fuck's sake! I touched GAVIN'S penis! In all of our talks about this stupid list, we never discussed the specifics. Like how to give a proper hand job. It was probably the worst thing he's ever experienced. How am I ever going to face him again?" I whine.

"Stop being so dramatic. It couldn't have been that bad. If you touch the penis, the penis will be happy. I did have one guy, though, who would only touch my penis with his thumb and forefinger. Like he was trying to milk a cow. I'm not saying I have a ginormous penis or anything, but it's definitely bigger than a cow's teat. Tell me you didn't milk his penis," Rocco begs.

"It probably would have gone better if I had. He actually said 'ouch' and 'be careful.' I think I pulled too hard."

"What the fuck were you doing with his dick? You know those things need to stay attached, right?" Rocco questions me in horror.

"SHUT UP! I told you, I have no fucking experience with this shit. I just reached in and started yanking on it."

"I think my balls just ran away in fear. Oh look, there they go, right out the front door. GOOD-BYE, BOYS!" Rocco shouts with a wave to the door of the bar.

"I hate you. I really hate you," I complain.

Rocco laughs and pats me on the back. "No you don't. You love me. You're just so cute when you get mad. I promise, no more comments about your inadequate dick handling. Carry on."

I down the rest of my glass of wine and take a deep breath, determined to get through this horrific story quickly so I never have to speak of it ever again.

Getting up from the couch, I walked into the kitchen to see what was taking Gavin so long. I heard whispering coming from the other side of the fridge, so I headed in that direction. I really should have stopped after three beers. Alcohol gave me liquid courage, but I maybe had a bit too much at that point. All I could think about was ripping Gavin's clothes off of him.

I heard Gavin say *balls* and figured he was on the phone with work. *Is it weird that I'm strangely turned on every time Gavin talks about what he does for a living?*

Walking around the edge of the fridge, Gavin looked up at me in surprise with his phone still pressed against his ear. He didn't say a word as I moved in closer to him, but I saw his eyes flash back and forth between my boobs and my face. Sweet! Maybe the list Rocco made was actually working. Showing more cleavage was a great idea after all. Wait. What if he wasn't looking at my boobs? What if he was looking at a mole I have on my chest? Did I have a mole on my chest? Son of a bitch, what if it was a hairy mole and he was so overcome with disgust that all he could think about was this fucking mole?! Or it could be food. Oh holy Jesus, what if I had a piece of leftover pizza stuck to my chest? I could play it off, tell him I put a slice of pepperoni there so he could lick it off.

I decided to do the most logical thing and just pretended like I didn't have a hairy piece of mole pepperoni sticking to my tits.

Gavin slowly lowered the phone from his ear and continued to stare at me without saying a word.

"Are you done with work stuff?" I asked.

He nodded his head.

"We kissed the other night."

Might as well divert his attention from my pizza boobs.

He nodded again.

Fuck! Why won't he just say something! At this point, I might actually prefer it if he points and says, "HOLY MOLEY!"

I tried again. "What were you feeling when we kissed?"

I leaned in closer, hoping to distract him by my proximity. It didn't work. He looked away from my face and right down the front of my shirt.

"I HAVE NUTS!" he shouted suddenly.

Glancing down, I realized he was unzipping his pants. *Well, this escalated quickly. I guess we can ignore the talk and just go right for the good stuff.* I wrapped my hand around the back of his head and pulled his face to mine, slamming my lips against his.

I took my other hand and quickly tried to shove it down the front of his pants, but with my eyes closed, I misjudged where I was going and punched him in the stomach.

"OOOF!" he blurts against my lips. "I'm sorry, I'm sorry! I shouldn't have unzipped my pants. I have no idea why I did that! Don't hit me again!" Gavin said in a rush.

Shit! I don't want him to think I'm offended!

"I totally didn't mean to do that. I'm going to stick my hand down your pants now," I warned him.

"Oh my God," he mumbled as I cut him off with my lips and slid my hand inside his boxer briefs.

Oh fuck. I'm touching his penis. My hand is on his penis. I was so excited I didn't even realize how hard I was squeezing his penis.

And thinking about it just makes me squeeze it even harder.

"Ouch!" Gavin winced and pulled away from my mouth.

Instead of letting up, I jerked in surprise when he shouted, bringing his penis with me. So basically, I was choking the life out of this thing and trying to detach it from his body. *WHAT THE FUCK AM I DOING?!*

"It's okay. It's fine. Just be careful," Gavin said before pulling me back to him and kissing me.

Be careful. I can do this. Just pretend it's a cat. Nice kitty. Nice, soft kitty.

Gavin pulled away again and I growled in frustration. I wanted his lips on me and he kept moving them.

"You're petting my penis," he stated.

Well, I WAS until you stopped me. QUIT IT!

"Stop talking," I told him.

I couldn't think when he talked. The sound of his voice made me feel all warm and gooey, and I wanted to do this right. I wanted him to feel good and maybe realize that by touching his penis, I love him.

Picturing every porn I've seen in my mind, except that weird one that Aunt Jenny showed me with people dressed up as Smurfs, I wrapped my hand around him and started moving it up and down slowly. Gavin groaned and closed his eyes, letting his head fall back against the wall.

I realized that we were wedged between the fridge and the counter, and it wasn't the most ideal location to be doing this, but I didn't care. This is happening right the fuck now.

Leaning forward, I placed my lips on his neck and let my tongue taste his skin. He groaned again and I picked up the pace with my hand, moving it up and down his smooth shaft.

I wondered if that slut Brooklyn really did all the things she said she did with him? I wanted to cut that whore for ever laying a finger on my Gavin. I didn't realize I was channeling my anger to Gavin's penis until he whimpered in pain. *Dammit. Focus, Charlotte! There are better ways to mark your territory than by dismembering the man you love.* Securing my lips to his neck once again, I nibbled and bit his skin before sucking it into my mouth.

There, take that, you skanky piece of trash! He's mine!

"Oh shit, Charlotte. Slow down," Gavin begged, wrapping one of his hands around my wrist and sliding the other into the edge of my jeans by my hip.

I ignored his warning and moved my hand harder and faster, up and down his length. He tried to hold my wrist tighter to get me to slow down, but I wasn't having any of that. His hips thrusted into my hand, and it was the hottest thing I ever felt.

I am NOT stopping.

"Charlotte … Jesus … .I'm gonna … oh holy shit fuck …"

I felt his fingers graze the skin of my hip, and I wanted more than anything for him to just dive right in like I did with him. I wanted him to touch me, but I was pretty sure he was beyond rational thought right now. His fingers tangled into the fabric of my thong resting on my hip, and he clutched it so tightly the fabric ripped.

He's going to come! I'm totally making him come! This is the best day ever!

"Okay, so aside from the fact that you pet his dick like a cat, I don't see what the problem is," Rocco says when I pause with my story. "You might be surprised to know that I've had my dick pulled by a few of the ladies back in the day. You're not the only one who has no idea how to use one of those things. At least you got the hang of it."

"Sure, I got into a nice rhythm and he finished pretty fast. That was awesome. But in porn, they don't tell you what to do when it's all over. The scene just ends and there's no cleanup involved," I complain.

Rocco stares at me for a few minutes and then the light bulb comes on and his eyes widen.

"Oh dear God. What did you do with the jizz in your hand? Charlotte! What did you do with the jizz?!"

Biting my lip and squeezing my eyes closed so I don't have to see Rocco's face, I blurt it out quickly.

"I pulled my hand out of his pants and then sort of whipped my hand in his general direction to get it off. Then I just turned and walked out of his apartment."

Opening my eyes, I see Rocco with his hand over his mouth trying to contain his laughter.

"Oh no you didn't. Oh, Charlotte. You Spidermanned the one you love."

Chapter 14

~ Cat Fight ~

"Ava, are you home?" I shout into my parents' house as I walk through the front door.

Moving into the living room, I see a flash of naked, white ass streaking down the hall to the guest bathroom and Ava rearranging her skirt on the couch. Not one piece of her long, dark brown hair is out of place, and she looks like she just stepped off the pages of a fashion magazine. Her make-up is flawless and her blue skirt and matching tank top are perfectly pressed. Not at all what someone should look like who was just doing what I KNOW she was doing.

"Oh my God. Ava! Were you having sex on mom and dad's couch? That's disgusting. I sit on that couch," I complain.

She rolls her eyes. "Fuck off, twat. I laid a blanket down."

Glancing underneath her, I see the blanket in question.

"Son of a bitch! That's the comforter from my bed!" I yell

with a stomp of my foot.

"Ooooh, the older sister. This is like a porn dream come true. Can I be on the bottom?"

My head whips around to the door of the hallway and I see Tyler standing there buttoning his shirt.

"Oh my God. I'm going to have to burn that blanket now. And the couch."

Tyler finishes with his shirt and walks over to the couch, plopping down next to Ava and throwing his arm over her shoulder.

"Don't worry, Charlotte, I only got a little Tyler juice on your blanket. It's all good."

Ava shoves Tyler away from her and gets up from the couch. "I'm finished with you. You can leave now."

Tyler pouts and stares up at her. "Babe, that wounds me. I'm delicate after my run-in with Claire the other day. Be gentle."

Ava rolls her eyes and walks over to the door, opening it up and pointing outside. "Aunt Claire made you wash her kitchen floor with a toothbrush and mow the lawn with a pair of scissors. Go away or I'll make you gargle toilet water."

Tyler stands up and saunters over to her. "Ooooh, kinky. I like that. Until next time. Unless you gave me the clap. In that case, call first."

Tyler whistles as he walks out the door and Ava slams it shut behind him.

"I cannot believe you had sex with that thing," I tell her as she comes back into the living room.

"You should be thanking me right now, you whore. I took one for the team to see if I could get any information on Gavin after you threw a web of spooge on his shirt," she complains.

"God dammit! Will you stop bringing that up!"

Ava shrugs, gathers up the blanket, and throws it behind the couch before taking a seat. "I'm sorry, but that's some funny shit. You threw sperm at him. You're like the creepy guy in Silence of the Lambs, throwing goo through the jail cell bars. At least you didn't hit him in the face with it."

I should have never trusted Ava with this information. She's my sister and I love her, but she never lets shit go. She still brings up every single time I've ever tattled on her when we were growing up in casual conversation. She's got the memory of an elephant and can tell everyone who asks the exact date, time, and outfit we were both wearing when I told Mom that she drew a picture of a penis in crayon on the back of my bedroom door when she was twelve.

"Since you decided to be a slut for the cause, tell me you at least got some information out of Tyler," I beg, taking a seat next to her.

"Tyler shouts the names of My Little Ponies when he comes. And he makes horse noises with his lips when he's going down on me."

My mouth opens and I gag.

"I know. It's weird. But it was kind of hot. If you ever tell anyone I said that I will smother you in your sleep," she warns.

"Can we get back to more pressing matters please? What did

he say about Gavin?"

Ava sighs and leans back into the couch. "He didn't say much. That boy is loyal; I'll give him that. Every time I asked him about Gavin he would just say, 'Well, what does Charlotte think?' It was annoying. I even tried asking him when his penis was in my mouth, figuring it would distract him."

Eeew, I really don't want to picture Tyler's penis in ANYONE'S mouth, especially my sister's. He's a good-looking guy I guess. Around six feet tall with surfer blonde hair and blue eyes, but as soon as he opens his mouth it ruins everything.

"How do you talk with a penis in your mouth?" I question.

"It takes some practice. You have to know how to roll your *r*'s and really enunciate. I'm pretty good, but he still thought when I asked if Gavin liked you I said, 'Muff diving dike harlot.' He thought I was telling him I'm a slutty lesbian. It took me fifteen minutes to get him to focus after that."

Fuck! How in the hell am I going to find out how Gavin feels about what happened between us? Tyler was my last hope.

"I have a great idea. How about you find some balls and just tell Gavin how you really feel?" Ava suggests with a glare at me.

"Yeah, because that would go over really well. 'Oh hey, Gavin. So, I know we grew up together and we've been best friends since we were little. We usually tell each other everything but here's something new. Every time I'm around you I want to climb your face like a tree. Oh and you know how all my friends dared me to kiss you at the bar last week? Yeah, totally false. I just made that up because I've been dying to stick my tongue down your throat since

I was twelve. No, please, stop laughing so hard. I'm serious.'"

I end my tirade and stare back at Ava.

"Yeah, that's probably pretty accurate. Okay, so what's left on Rocco's list?" she asks.

I heave out a sigh and throw my head back against the couch. "Dress up like a slutty school girl, get a flat tire and call him for help, take him to a sporting event and pretend like I know what's going on, and take naked pictures of him. But obviously that suggestion was for Rocco's benefit."

Ava shakes her head sadly at me. "Rocco isn't going to be able to keep his gayness contained for much longer. Did you know he called Dad the other day and asked him if he wanted to go to a game? Dad thought maybe he'd misjudged him and felt bad. Then Rocco told him the game was drag queen bingo. I think Dad put a hit out on him."

I hear the front door open and a few seconds later my mom walks into the living room.

"Why does it smell like sex in here? Ava, shouldn't you be at work?" she asks with her hands on her hips.

"I'm on my lunch break," Ava says casually.

Mom looks at her watch. "It's four o'clock."

"Snack break?" Ava replies with a shrug.

"AVA!"

"Um, I'm sick," she says, adding in a cough for good measure.

"I swear to Christ if you left work to come home and have sex in my house, I will stop paying your cell phone bill," Mom threatens.

"Oooooh, not the cell phone bill!" I reply in mock seriousness. "Careful, Ava. Mom's got her stern face on."

Ava and I both giggle while Mom stands there tapping her foot angrily.

"You two are both adults, so I have no problem saying this to you right now. You're a bunch of dicks."

"Mom, you said that to us when we were eight," I remind her.

"Well, now I really mean it. Charlotte, how's the job search coming along?" she asks as she takes her shoes off and moves into the room to sit in the chair across from us.

"Lousy. No one is hiring," I complain.

"You know you can always come and work for Seduction and Snacks," she reminds me.

My mom has been asking me to work for her ever since I was old enough to know what sex toys were. A part of me would love to go into the family business. I love my family and it would be awesome to work with them. The only thing holding me back right now is Gavin. It's bad enough that our families are close and we see each other a lot. If whatever this is between us completely implodes, not only would I have to see him at family get-togethers, I'd have to work side-by-side with him every day. What if he marries Brooklyn and I have to watch her coming into the office every day for a quickie? I can't work under those conditions. It would be best if I just find a job elsewhere.

"Mom, I can't work at Seduction and Snacks," I tell her.

"Why? What's so bad about working there? Do you have vibrator anxiety? I thought we went over this on your eighteenth birthday when I bought you that starter kit," Mom says with concern in her voice.

Both an upside AND a downside to having a mother who owns a sex toy store: she always wants to talk to you about sex and buys you vibrators for every holiday. And usually whips them out at the dinner table when you have guests over.

"Mom, I am not afraid of vibrators. If I'm not mistaken, you used to put a vibrator under my crib mattress to get me to sleep when I was a baby. You're lucky I don't turn narcoleptic every time I hear one buzzing."

"Well, if that's not the problem, what is? Seduction and Snacks is a very good company to work for. There are so many options for you to choose from with a degree in Communications," she tells me.

"I think you should be more concerned with the fact that you and Dad forked over ninety-thousand dollars in tuition for this fuckernutter to get a degree in talking when she can't even manage to say three little words to a certain someone." Ava crosses her arms over her chest and looks at me smugly.

"AVA!"

"WHAT?!" Mom and I both shout at the same time.

"Oh for fuck's sake, Charlotte. This is getting annoying. Mom, Charlotte is in love with Gavin," Ava states, crossing her arms in front of her.

"WHAT?!" Mom shouts again, looking back and forth between us with wide eyes.

"I am going to reach down your throat and rip out your

ovaries, you fat cow!" I yell at her.

"Oh, I'm sorry, was that a secret?" Ava asks me, batting her eyelashes.

"AVA HAD SEX WITH TYLER!" I scream, pointing my finger at her.

"WHAT?!"

Either Mom's head is about to explode or she's having a stroke and can only speak one word. Whatever it is, I'm not about to let Ava win this shit. I'm small, but I'm scrappy. Even when we were little and she would get pissed at me and pull my hair, I always finished the fights and had her screaming for mom within seconds.

"You fucking HAG!" Ava screams at me. "Charlotte tried to give Gavin a pearl necklace!"

"Ava likes it when Tyler shouts My Little Pony names instead of hers!"

Before I can come up with another insult, Ava launches herself at me and grabs onto my hair. She yanks it hard and I scream in pain, reaching my own hand up and clutching onto a chunk of her dark brown locks. We're smacking, pulling, biting, screaming, and kicking for only a few seconds before Mom dives on top of us, trying to pull us apart.

"GIRLS! That's enough!" she yells, grabbing onto both of our arms as they flail all around, trying to gain purchase.

"Hey, sweet thing, I think I dropped my wallet under the-"

All three of us immediately stop screaming and fighting and turn our heads to the door as Tyler stands there with his bottom lip quivering.

"Mom AND daughters ... I never thought this day would come. God does exist."

Chapter 15

~ You're a Labia ~

"Seriously, Charlotte. You need to watch this. It's goats screaming like humans," Molly tells me in a fit of giggles as she stares at her iPhone.

Molly is nineteen and the youngest out of the three of us girls. Where Ava and I take after our dad with dark hair and dark eyes, Molly is the spitting image of my mom with her long blonde hair and spitfire personality.

"I don't have time for that shit right now, Molls. I need a sharp object that will poke a hole in a tire," I tell her distractedly as I look through all of the cupboards in the kitchen.

After our catfight a few days ago, Ava and I called a truce and she suggested I go with the whole flat tire item on the list next. Guys like a damsel in distress. Rocco assured me that it would be a good way to make Gavin feel like a man. He's under the impression that Gavin is probably more embarrassed about what happened last week than I am. I find that hard to believe, but whatever. He hasn't called or sent me a text since it happened and it's freaking me out.

"No, really. Come here and watch this. It's a Taylor Swift video and during the chorus, goats scream. Oh my God, this is the best thing I've ever seen," Molly says in between hysterical laughter.

Opening the silverware drawer, I pull out the largest butcher knife I can find.

"Jesus, put the knife away. I'll stop playing goat screaming videos," Molly says in a panic as she comes up behind me, staring nervously at the knife in my hand.

Rolling my eyes at her, I close the drawer with my hip and grab my purse off of the counter.

"I swear to God you never listen to anything that goes on in this house."

Molly follows behind me as I make my way to the front door.

"Oh, I heard all about you trying to beat the shit out of Ava. Why do I miss all of the good stuff?" Molly complains.

"Because you're in school. Or you're supposed to be. Why aren't you at school right now?"

Molly is five years younger than me and from an early age, she loved helping Aunt Claire out in the kitchen. Right now she's in school full-time earning her degree in Culinary Arts so she can be a pastry chef for one of Aunt Claire's stores.

"It's midterms week. I only have to go to class for my tests.

So, remind me again why you're taking a knife with you to meet Gavin? I don't think gutting him like a fish will convince him that he loves you," Molly says with a laugh.

"No, but hopefully slashing my tires will."

Molly shakes her head at me. "I still don't understand how you could possibly be in love with Gavin. I mean, this is GAVIN we're talking about. He used to take the heads off of all of our Barbie's and then staple them to the ceiling. And you two used to fight constantly when we were kids. How many times did Mom and Aunt Claire have to break you guys up before you killed each other?"

She's right. We hated each other as kids. I don't even know why we didn't like each other. Every time we were in the same room together, someone wound up crying.

"That dress looks funny on you," Gavin told me, grabbing my favorite *I can be a teacher* Barbie from my hands and then throwing it across the room.

"You're a dumb stupid head. Go pick up my Barbie right now," I said with a stomp of my foot.

"You're such a baby. I can't believe you called me a dumb stupid head," Gavin replied with a laugh.

"I'm not a baby. YOU'RE a baby!" I shouted.

"I'm nine. That's practically an adult."

"Fine, then you're dumb stupid adult!" I yelled angrily.

"You're a labia," Gavin replied.

"What's a labia? That's dumb."

Gavin shrugged. "I heard it the other day. My mom said it's a rare fish that no one ever talks about."

"I want a labia," I told him.

"You can't have a labia. You ARE a labia. Labia face," he said, turning his back on me and walking away.

I was so angry that I hurtled my six-year-old body at him and wrapped my arms around him from behind, tackling him to the ground.

"GAAAAAAAAAAAAAAH MY NUTS!" Gavin screamed in pain as we crashed to the floor and he flung me off of him.

I stood up quickly and stared down at him angrily.

"You're mean. I don't like you."

Gavin scrambled up off of the ground and before I knew it, he charged at me and slammed his head into my hip, knocking us both back on the ground.

We were both screaming and crying when my mom and Aunt Liz came running into the room.

"What the hell is going on?" Aunt Claire shouted as she picked Gavin up off of the floor and my mom helped me up.

"SHE HURT MY NUTS!" Gavin cried, pointing at me.

"HE CRASHED HIS HEAD INTO MY NOO-NOO-COW!" I wailed, holding my hands between my legs.

"Jesus God. He head-butted her in the vagina," my mom muttered.

"I hope these two get married some day or this is just going to get worse," Aunt Claire replied.

Opening the door, I lift up my arm and wave good-bye to Molly with the knife. "Wish me luck. If this flat tire thing doesn't work, I might have to punch him in the nuts."

"I have no idea what that means, but have fun with that. Bring me home some mint chocolate chip ice cream."

Thirty minutes later, after I called Gavin and told him my *dilemma*, I'm standing next to my car on the side of the road listening to the hiss of the air leaving the tire. I may have been a little overzealous in my stabbing. There's no way Gavin is going to believe my car just got a flat on its own. He's a guy. Guys know these things. I don't have time to worry about that, though. I see his car pulling off the side of the road right behind mine. Leaning against the hood, I try to look as sexy as possible. Rocco suggested I pretend like I'm in a porno. Ultimate guy fantasy: a woman having car problems on the side of the road.

Gavin gets out of his car and walks up to me with a smile. "Flat tire, huh?"

Shit. He already knows. Time to distract him.

"Hey there, handsome. I could use a little help pumping myself back up," I tell him in my best Marilyn Monroe voice.

Gavin looks at me quizzically. "Are you getting sick? You're voice sounds funny."

Fucking Rocco.

Clearing my throat, I turn away from him and walk up to the front tire. "I don't know what happened. I was driving home when all of a sudden I had a hard time steering. My car was swerving all over the place. I was so scared."

Gavin glances down at the tire, then back up at me and doesn't say a word.

Son of a bitch! Do cars lose control when they get a flat tire?? I should have googled it.

"Aww, you're okay now. It's totally normal. Cars always do that with a flat tire," Gavin tells me.

Oh thank God.

"So, do you want a lift home or something?" he asks.

"Uh, I kind of thought you could just change the tire," I tell him.

Gavin nods his head. "Right, right. Change the tire. I can totally do that."

He turns and walks around me, opening up the door to the backseat and sticking his head in.

"What are you doing?"

Pulling his head back out, he turns and looks at me. "Changing the tire."

"I think the stuff's in the trunk," I tell him in confusion.

He laughs awkwardly and slams the door closed. "Oh, yeah. I totally knew that. I was just checking to make sure you didn't do any damage ... to the ... backseat and stuff."

While he quickly walks to the trunk, I reach in through the driver's side window and hit the trunk release button. Moving to the back of the car, I see him standing there just staring into the trunk.

"Everything is under that floor mat," I tell him, pointing to the middle of the trunk.

"I know. I was just ... um ... assessing the situation. Thinking about my plan of attack," he replies, reaching into the trunk and flipping back the mat.

I watch as he leans in and grabs the tire iron, flipping it up in the air casually as he turns and smiles at me. He reaches his arm out to catch it as it comes back down, but instead of catching it, he smacks his hand against it and the thing goes flying out into the middle of the road. His smile falls and he races over to quickly pick it up.

With his head down and the tire iron clutched tightly to his chest, he walks right by me and up to the tire. I'm pretty sure he's trying to look cool, and I am not about to call him out on it since I stuck a fucking butcher knife into my tire to get him here.

Squatting down on his knees next to the tire, he attaches one end of the iron to a nut and starts to turn it.

"Um, you need to jack the car up first," I remind him.

"I know that. I always loosen the screws first."

"They're called lug nuts."

"Well, where I come from, we call them screws."

"We both come from Ohio. I'm pretty sure they call them lug

nuts everywhere," I say with a laugh.

"Are you trying to tell me how to change a tire? I know how to change a tire," he complains with a huff, grunting as he puts all of his muscle into trying to loosen the nut.

Oh my God. He doesn't know how to change a tire.

"You don't know how to change a tire," I mutter.

Shit! Rocco is going to kill me. This is so not going to make Gavin feel like a man. I need to shut the fuck up.

Gavin drops the tire iron to the ground with a *clang* and stands up, stalking over to me.

"I totally know how to change a tire," he argues, as we stand toe-to-toe.

"Fine. What's the part on the tire where the air goes?" I question.

He purses his lips and stares down at me. "It's an air-tube-put-inner-thing."

It's kind of cute that he's trying to act like he knows what he's talking about. But it's also a little irritating. I have a flat tire and he was supposed to be the big man and fix it for me so he could feel better about what happened the other night. My dad taught me when I was five how to change a tire.

"Actually, it's a valve stem," I tell him with a smile.

"Whatever! It has nothing to do with changing the actual tire so who cares?!" he complains.

"I can't believe you don't know how to change a tire. You're a guy and you have a penis. You should have been born knowing how to change a tire!"

Gavin puts his hands on his hips and glares at me. "Yeah, well you're a girl and you have a vagina. Does that mean you can waltz over to that field over there, squat down, and pop out a baby?"

The way we're arguing reminds me of when we were little. We haven't done this in a long time. It always pissed me off when I was young. Now it turns me on. Gavin is so hot standing here in front of me on the side of a deserted road. My eyes move away from his, and I find myself staring at his lips.

I open my mouth to fire off a smart-ass reply to his vagina comment when I'm suddenly pulled up against him and his mouth crashes down to mine.

Maybe this whole flat tire thing actually worked.

Chapter 16

~ Children of the Corn ~

Gavin ends the kiss before I'm ready for it to be finished and pulls away from me. He opens up the back seat of the car and jerks his head. "Get in."

I don't even hesitate. I have no idea why I'm getting in the back seat of my car, and I don't care as long as it involves more kissing. Quickly crawling into the car, I turn around to find Gavin getting in beside me. I grab onto the front of his shirt as he slams the door closed behind him and pull him against me, our mouths colliding so hard that our teeth clank together.

"Ouch!"

God dammit! Once again I'm putting him in pain. At least it wasn't his penis this time.

Moving back slowly this time, I press my lips to his. His tongue eases its way inside my mouth, and I can't stop the groan when I feel it slide against my own. One of his arms wraps around my waist and he slides my butt across the seat, leaning his body against mine to get me to lie back. All of this happens really quickly, though, and my head smacks against the window.

"Fucking hell!" I shout, reaching up to rub the back of my head.

"Shit! I'm sorry, are you okay?" he asks in a panic.

"I'm fine. Totally fine," I reassure him. I don't care if I have a head wound that is spraying blood all over the interior of my car; we aren't stopping.

Scooting myself lower onto the seat this time, Gavin turns his body and moves between my legs, bumping his own head on the ceiling.

Seriously? Can we catch a fucking break here?

Twisting and turning our bodies to try and get into a comfortable position, there's a bunch of swearing, more body parts smacking into various pieces of the car's interior, and the windows are starting to fog up from our exertion. This is so not as hot as it is in the movies. Why the fuck are back seats so small?

After ten minutes of us scrambling around, we're finally both on our sides facing each other, my back pressed up against the seat.

"I should turn on some music or something," Gavin tells me as he starts to move away from me.

Wrapping my arms around his neck, I pull him back to me. "Don't even think about moving or it will take us another hour to find comfortable positions."

Gavin laughs, moving his hand up to brush a strand of hair out of my eye.

"Are we going to talk about last week?" he asks.

I shake my head. "I really don't want to talk right now. You should just take your pants off."

Gavin stares at me blankly for a minute and I wonder if maybe that was too much. Before I can tell him I was just kidding so it's not awkward, he quickly reaches down and undoes his jeans, sliding them right off of his body and then ripping his shirt off of his head in five seconds flat, tossing everything onto the floor next to us. I feel like it's only fair that I do the same. I pull my shirt off and lift my hips, shimmying out of my skirt and kicking it up to the front seat.

"Oh my God. You're naked," Gavin whispers in awe.

At least I think it's awe. It could be shock. Or fear. Fuck, I hope it's not fear.

"Do you want me to put my clothes back on?"

"Don't you dare put your clothes back on. This is the best day EVER," he replies. He places his palm flat on my chest and runs it down the front of my body. I swallow nervously as he touches me. Gavin has never touched me like this. NO ONE has ever touched me like this. He's right. This is the best day ever.

Leaning up, I press my lips to his. He immediately deepens the kiss and pulls me underneath him. Wrapping my legs around his hips, I pull him against me and holy fuck is he hard. He's hard because of me. I mean, I know it happened before, but I was touching his penis. If a feather touched his penis he'd probably get hard. I haven't even touched him yet. He wants me and I want him and this is totally going to happen right now. I don't care if we're in the back seat of a fucking Honda.

Okay, I totally care that we're in the back seat of my shitty car. This is like the worst cliché in history. Girl loses virginity in the back seat. What if someone drives by? What if someone looks in the window? Gavin is still kissing me and his hands are pushing down my underwear and all I can think about is someone staring in the window. I stopped next to a cornfield. Are the Children of the Corn gathering around the car getting ready to kill us?! He who walks behind the rows!

"Did you just call me Malachai?" Gavin asks, pulling his head away from me.

It's never a good idea to call a guy by another man's name when you're about to have sex, even if it's a homicidal maniac dressed like an Amish kid.

"Ha! What? No! I said, 'May I lick..I," I fumble.

"If you want to lick yourself, go right ahead." He laughs. "That might be kind of hot."

Pushing all thoughts of Malachai staring at us with a bloody sickle in his hand, I help Gavin remove his boxer briefs, and then he helps me slide my underwear off. I quickly pull his body back down to mine.

This time when he kisses me, I stop thinking. All I do is feel. His hands run over every inch of my body he can reach, and before I know it, I feel his fingers sliding between my legs. While his tongue tangles with mine and his fingers ghost over my clit, I sigh into his mouth and try not to think about the fact that I've never gotten a Brazilian. I keep everything nice and tidy down there, so it's not like he's going to get his fingers tangled or anything, but maybe I should have taken my mother up on her offer to go with her when she went to *her* appointment the other day. Something about going somewhere with my mother where we're both naked from the waist down, spread-eagle on a table, and letting a stranger paw around down there with hot wax didn't sound appealing. Go figure.

Oh sweet Jesus his fingers …

Working for a sex toy manufacturer has definitely given him some skills. He uses just the right amount of pressure as his fingers gently circle my clit, and I can't stop the sounds escaping from my mouth as he slowly pushes one inside me.

My best friend is diddling me. This is totally happening!

"Fuck, you feel amazing," Gavin whispers against my lips as he holds his finger still inside of me and moves his thumb back and forth right where I need him.

Keep talking. Holy hell, keep talking.

"You're so wet and soft and it's so cool you don't shave or wax."

Wait, what? That's not hot.

"Did you just say I'm hairy?" I question on a gasp as he adds a second finger to the first.

I have a hairy wildebeest vagina. That's what he's saying, isn't it?

"What?! No! That's not what I meant!" he quickly adds as his fingers continue sliding in and out of me.

This feels good. Fuck no, this feels AMAZING. But all I can think about right now is that he thinks my vagina feels like an English sheepdog. All that hair falling down over the top of its eyes so it can't see where it's going. You know, if my vagina had eyes. It could be a scary movie: If the Vagina had Eyes. Rogue vaginas pissed off because they're so hairy, hiding in abandoned houses, waiting to bring down their wrath on unsuspecting townspeople. Wait, didn't Big Bird have a dog like that named Barkley on Sesame Street? Gavin is going to start calling my vagina Barkley.

I'm so preoccupied with my sheepdog vagina that I don't immediately notice Gavin is reaching his one arm down to the floor; the arm that isn't busy reaching into the horror story that is my vagina. He fumbles around for a few seconds before coming back with a condom in his hand.

"I swear I don't always carry these around with me. Aunt Jenny gave them to me a few weeks ago and they've been in my wallet ever since," he reassures me as he sees me staring at the little foil packet in his hand.

"I'm fine. It's totally fine. Of course you should carry condoms. You need those for sex. The sex that you have. The sex that everyone has," I ramble.

Everyone but me. Oh shit, I should really come clean and tell him I've never done this before. I don't have time to confess that little white lie, though, because he's back to kissing me again and putting on the condom at the same time. This is happening.

He positions himself at my opening, and since his nimble fingers got me nice and wet before Barkley made an appearance, he starts to slide right in like it's no big deal. This is really happening and it's a big deal and oh my holy fuck JESUS MOTHER OF FIRE BURNING HELL THIS HURTS!

My thighs clamp down like vises on his hips, and I squeeze my eyes closed as he pushes the rest of the way inside me.

Ouch, ouch, ouch, ouch, fucking holy shit ouch.

"Holy shit. What the fuck? Oh my God. Charlotte, why the hell didn't you say something?!" Gavin curses as he holds himself still and winces like he's the one in pain. FUCK YOUR MOTHER! The only pain being had right now is by me and my vagina.

"Oh shit, oh shit, oh shit, oh my God I'm sorry. Are you okay? WHY DIDN'T YOU SAY SOMETHING?!" Gavin shouts.

"Telling you I'm a virgin is not exactly romantic," I fire back.

"God dammit! The only reason I even had sex with Shelly in high school was because I thought you had sex with DJ! Fuck! Your dad is going to kill me!" he complains.

"Can we NOT talk about my father right now?" I shout.

"We can't talk about your father, we can't talk about you being a virgin, what the fuck CAN we talk about?!" he yells.

"Are we really going to argue about this right now when your penis is inside of me?!" I scream back.

We lie there, breathing heavy and staring at one another, until Gavin's shoulders droop and he leans his forehead down against mine.

"You should have told me," he whispers before pulling back and kissing my cheek. "I hurt you."

He kisses my cheek, my nose, my eyes, and finally my lips. "We should stop. It shouldn't be like this … in the back seat of your car. You should have music and candles and flowers."

"We are not stopping. I'm okay now, I swear. The deed is done. I am no longer a virgin, thank you very much," I remind him.

"I want this to be good for you," he pleads.

"It IS good for me. I swear."

I pull him back to me and kiss him. After a few minutes, he begins to move against me and this time, I'm vocal with my *ouch*.

"Okay, maybe it isn't going to be THAT good. I'm sorry. It's not you, it's me. We're parked next to a corn field and I'm pretty sure there are killer children out there waiting to bust in the windows and stab us," I tell him.

"I knew you said Malachai before. And don't worry, I can totally fix this situation," Gavin says.

I start to protest as he moves away from me again, but he just reaches down to the floor and fumbles around again for a few seconds. He pulls his arm back and in his hand is the world's tiniest bullet vibrator.

"Did you just pull a vibrator out of your jeans?"

"Yes, yes I did. See? My job is TOTALLY awesome," he says with a smile as he presses a button and the little silver ball fires up.

"Don't guys feel like less of a man if they have to use a vibrator on a woman?" I question.

"If you have an orgasm, that's all that matters to me. And you WILL have an orgasm. Ten out of ten women surveyed got off with this little guy," he tells me, sliding his hand between us.

"It's so hot when you talk shop," I tell him with a groan as he gently presses the bullet to my clit.

"Holy hell, make that eleven out of eleven women," I moan as he holds the bullet in place and slowly starts to move inside me.

It only takes me thirty seconds to have my first orgasm with a guy. And not just any guy—Gavin. And luckily, he doesn't take after his best friend and shout the names of My Little Pony when he comes during sex; he just shouts my name.

Chapter 17

~ Numb Vagina ~

"I want to try something," Gavin tells me later that night as we lie curled up together on his bed.

All in all, losing my virginity went pretty well, if I do say so myself. There was no awkward silence after it was over and nothing felt weird at all. It just felt … right. Everything feels right, aside from the fact that I had sex with my best friend and I haven't come clean yet about what I did to get us to this point. Gavin assumes I broke up with Rocco. Gavin doesn't know Rocco is my gay fake boyfriend and that I used Rocco just to make him jealous. How in the hell does one even start an admission like that? I need more time to figure this out before I tell him. Not a lot of time, just enough to make him fall madly in love with me and not care about the fact that I deceived him.

Gavin's palm runs up the inside of my thigh and I forget all about my fake boyfriend.

"I'm pretty sure you already tried that and it was a success." I laugh as he pushes my skirt out of the way and runs his fingertips along the edge of my underwear.

Kissing my cheek, he scoots his body down the bed and situates himself between my legs with his chin resting on my thigh. I watch his face as he stares at his fingers that continue to lightly skim over my underwear. My breath catches at his fierce concentration. He places a kiss on the inside of my thigh and then kisses his way up my leg, his fingers working their way under the edge of my underwear.

"What are you doing?" I whisper, following it up with a soft moan when he pulls my underwear to the side and then presses his lips right to my clit.

"Shh, just close your eyes," he tells me.

I have no choice when I feel his tongue dart out and circle me. My eyes close automatically and I arch my back as he licks me slowly.

So this is what I've been missing all these years. Holy Jesus.

He flattens his tongue and adds more pressure as he laps at me, like he's licking an ice cream cone. A vagina-flavored ice cream cone. Dairy Queen should put that on their menu. I would buy one for Gavin every single day.

He leans in closer and his lips join his tongue as he sucks and licks at me. It feels amazing … for about ten seconds. And then something weird happens. I know he's still down there because I've opened my eyes and I'm staring right at the top of his head between my legs, but suddenly, I don't feel him there anymore. I see his head moving, I witness his tongue darting out every few seconds as he goes to town on me, but I feel nothing. This isn't a dream is it? One of those weird wet dreams where you're just about to come and then wake up? What the fuck is going on?

Bringing my hands up to my face, I rub my palms roughly against my eyes, pulling them away and looking back down between my legs.

Okay, I'm awake and this isn't a dream. Am I suddenly paralyzed from the waist down? Oh holy shit, I've just gone paraplegic! I read about that happening to a woman in Brazil. She was just sitting there at the dinner table when all of a sudden she couldn't feel her legs, and now she's in a wheelchair. I DON'T WANT TO BE IN A WHEELCHAIR THE REST OF MY LIFE! Can oral sex cause paralysis?

Glancing over to the nightstand next to Gavin's bed, I see my iPhone. He's still busy so it's not like he's going to notice if I pull up Google on my phone. I can wiggle my toes so it can't be that bad.

Damn, I need a pedicure. I should schedule one for tomorrow.

I haven't made any encouraging noises in a few minutes; I should probably do that so Gavin doesn't think anything is amiss. I don't want him to never do this again. The first couple of seconds were mind-blowing. Maybe that's how oral sex is. You have to build up your tolerance for it. Maybe next time he does this, I'll feel it for thirty seconds. Then after that, a full minute.

Fuck, why did I put my phone so far out of reach?

"Oh yeah, just like that," I say, trying to keep the boredom out of my voice.

Do you have to wait a certain amount of time between orgasms? Maybe it's like swimming after eating. Lifting my arm up, I check my watch. It's been two hours since my last orgasm. Is that too soon to have another one?

"You taste so good, baby," Gavin says in between licks.

"Um, thanks?" I mutter.

It makes me feel all warm and fuzzy that he called me *baby*. Too bad that warmth doesn't travel to my vagina. What if it's broken? Did we break it when I lost my virginity?

"Mmmmm, yeah," I add in a breathy voice so he doesn't stop.

I've heard girls say that in pornos when they're getting oral. That sounds about right. I don't want to tell him to stop. What if he thinks I don't like what he's doing? I'm assuming I would like what he's doing if I could feel it. He's got a great tongue and he knows how to use it. I think.

Did I remember to turn off my straightening iron at home? Mom will kill me if I left that thing plugged in again.

Pretending like I'm really into this, I moan some more and start moving my hips, angling myself closer to the nightstand at the same time. Reaching my arm out slowly and making sure he's still preoccupied with my broken vagina, I grab my phone.

Gavin glances up at me and I quickly bring both of my hands to my chest, hiding my phone against me. "Oh yeah, that feels so good. Keep going."

He looks away from me and keeps on keeping on. I make sure

to continue moving my hips against him as I pull up the message app on my phone and send off a quick text to Molly.

Can u make sure I unplugged my straightener? Thx.

Pressing *send*, I glance down at Gavin. Man, he's really working it. Lips, tongue, fingers … if only I could feel it. My phone vibrates and I hide the noise with another loud moan while I check my messages.

It's unplugged. Whatcha doin? I'm bored. - Molly

"Don't stop," I mutter as I type a reply to my sister.

Eh, nothing much. I'm prob not going to be home till late.
Wanna go shopping tmrw?

I wonder if those shoes I wanted are still on sale at Macy's? They were so cute. Rocco would love them.

"Does it feel good? Are you close?" Gavin asks.

Quickly hiding my phone next to my hip, I smile down at him and nod my head. "Oh, so good. I'm really close."

He dives right back in, and when I'm sure he's not paying attention to me, I bring up Google and type in *numb vagina*.

Hmmm, sitting for long periods of time can cause a numb vagina. I didn't really sit down today for more than a few minutes, so that's not it. Nerve damage? Oh fuck no! What if I have damaged nerves? That doesn't sound like something easy to fix. "Hey, Doc, so I have this problem with broken nerves in my vagina. Get your scalpel, STAT!"

Certain yeast infection remedies have ingredients in them that soothe and cause numbing. That sounds about right, but I don't have cottage cheese vagina so that isn't it either. Clicking on the ingredients, I see one right at the top called Lysine. I've heard of that before. It's in a few of my plumping lip-glosses. Looking away from my phone and down at Gavin, I ponder this for a few minutes while he slurps and licks away at my vagina. I look back at my phone and then down at Gavin. Back and forth, back and forth.

SON OF A BITCH!

Throwing my phone down on the bed, I reach down with both hands and grab handfuls of Gavin's hair, pulling his head up.

"Hey, I wasn't finished yet," he complains.

"Did you put chapstick on before we got in bed?" I question.

He starts to move his head back down between my legs, but I clutch tighter and hold him in place.

His face scrunches up in pain as he stares at me. "Ouch! What? Chapstick? I don't know. I think so."

"Give me the chapstick."

Gavin looks at me like I've lost my mind. "I'm kind of in the middle of something here."

"GIVE ME THE CHAPSTICK!" I scream.

He scrambles up on his knees and fumbles in the back pocket of his jeans, quickly pulling out the small tube of MEDICATED

FUCKING CHAPSTICK.

Snatching it out of his hand, I read the ingredients.

"Active ingredients include camphor, cooling menthol, and phenol to relieve pain."

Gavin continues to stare at me while I shoot him a dirty look. "What?"

Sighing, I toss the chapstick at his chest. "You put on medicated chapstick before you went down on me."

I can see by the perplexed look on his face; he still doesn't get it.

"Tell me something. How did your lips feel right after you put on that chapstick?"

He thinks about this for a minute before responding. "Tingly. And then they numbed a little. I don't see what the problem is. I wanted to make sure my lips were nice and smooth before I did this. You should be thanking me."

Pulling my skirt down to cover myself, I scoot back on the bed until my back is against the headboard. "Say that again, out loud."

"You should be thanking me," he replies.

"No! Not that part. Sweet fucking hell ... the part about your lips."

He huffs at me and puts his hands on his hips. "Tingly. And then they numbed a lit ... Ohhhhhhhhhh."

He scrunches up his nose and winces at me. "So the whole time you couldn't—"

"Nope."

"And you were just making those noises so that—"

"Yep."

He lets out a huge sigh, crawling up the bed and then sitting next to me, our shoulders touching as we both lean against the headboard and stare blankly at the wall across the room.

"So, you wanna watch a movie or something?" he asks after a few minutes of silence.

I shrug. "Sure."

Well, it's good to know there's no awkwardness between us.

Chapter 18

~ Just Say No to Weird Sex ~

"I can't believe you had sex for the first time in the back seat of a car. You are such a whore," Ava tells me over the phone.

Even her annoying judgment can't put me in a bad mood right now. I had sex with Gavin. I had sex with Gavin and I had not one, but two orgasms. Whoever invented vibrators should be king of the world.

"Did you tell him you love him yet?" Ava questions as I pull into Gavin's driveway and check myself in the rearview mirror one last time before getting out of my car.

"No, not yet. There's one more thing I want to check off of my list before I do that," I inform her as I make my way up his front walk.

"Please tell me you aren't doing the food one," Ava begs.

"What? Why? That's a fun one. And now that we've got the

whole virginity thing out of the way, it will be awesome," I explain.

"Alright, fine. But don't say I didn't warn you," she tells me ominously before I roll my eyes and end the call.

Taking a deep breath, I reach my hand up and knock on his door. It's been a few days since the whole losing of the virginity thing, but I am happy to say that it hasn't been awkward between us at all. Gavin has been busy with work but we've talked on the phone every day. Before I finally admit that I love him and that I've spent all these months using a list Rocco made of things that would get him to fall in love with me, I want to have some fun.

The door opens and Gavin stands in the doorway, looking me up and down. "Nice coat."

He smiles at me and pushes the door open wider so I can come in. I borrowed one of Molly's white chef coats for the evening. And I'm not wearing anything underneath it.

"Are you cooking me dinner?"

I laugh and slide my hand into his, pulling him through the apartment and into his kitchen. "Nope, you know I can't cook. I've got something better planned," I tell him.

Stopping next to the fridge, I turn around to face him and unbutton the front of the coat until it's draped open and I'm just standing in a matching black lace bra and thong.

"Never mind. That coat sucks," he mutters as he stares at me.

He moves to come closer and I hold up my hand in front of him. "Nope. You just stay right there and close your eyes."

Gavin does as I ask and I quickly turn to the fridge and open the door.

"Are you making yourself a snack?" he asks with a laugh.

"Shush! Don't move and keep your eyes closed."

Bending down to stare into the fridge, I have a moment of doubt as I stare at the vast emptiness in front of me. How the hell am I going to do this? I knew I should have stopped at the store before I came here. Glancing around quickly, I grab the first bottle I see and quickly shut the door. Pulling up on the lid, I squirt the best upside down heart I can manage on my chest.

"Okay, you can open your eyes now," I tell him.

Gavin blinks his eyes open and stares. "Wow. Okay. Still hot. But what is that?" he asks, pointing to the heart.

"It's mustard. And you're going to lick it off me," I tell him with a confident smile.

This was such a better idea when I imagined it with chocolate sauce in my head.

"Mustard … I'm going to … yeah. That's hot. That's totally hot. I'm okay with this."

He walks up to me and gulps before lowering his head slower than I've ever seen him move. He scrunches up his face like he's in pain, and I'm starting to get a complex here.

"Is something wrong? I have a heart on my boobs that needs to be removed with your tongue," I remind him.

His mouth is hovering a few inches from my boobs, and he shakes his head back and forth quickly. "Nope. Nothing wrong. Nothing wrong at all. You are totally hot and I am going to lick this … mustard off of you. I'm going to do it and it's going to be awesome."

Right now it sounds like he's giving himself a pep talk instead of reassuring me that he's good.

I know it's not chocolate sauce, but come on! Half naked woman standing here! I close my eyes as he starts to move forward again and right when I feel his warm breath on my chest and anticipate the feel of his tongue against my skin, I hear a gagging sound. Popping my eyes open, I look down at him.

"Are you gagging right now? Oh my God, Gavin! You're totally gagging when your mouth is right by my boobs!" I shout.

"It's ... not ... your ... boobs! I ... love ... your ... boobs!" he yells, gagging in between each word as he backs away.

"I cannot believe you're gagging!" I tell him, stomping my foot.

"Oh God, I'm sorry! I hate ... mustard. Oh Jesus, I thought I could do this but I can't. It's ... mustard ... fuck ... mustard is ... uuugghh ... mustard."

"WILL YOU STOP SAYING *MUSTARD* IF IT MAKES YOU SICK?!" I shout, reaching for a towel on the counter and quickly wiping the mustard heart off of my chest.

"Why the hell do you have mustard in your fridge if you hate it?" I demand.

"I don't know! I'm a dude. Dudes always have mustard in their fridge!"

"There, is that better?" I ask, tossing the towel into the sink and holding my arms out.

"Yes, much better," he tells me with a sigh as he moves back toward me.

He wraps his arms around my waist and pulls me up against him. Just as soon as our bodies touch, he pushes me away and takes a step back.

"Nope, not better. I can still smell it. Oh Jesus, it's so mustardy!"

His hand is covering his mouth at this point and he's bent over at the waist. In an angry huff, I turn around and march back to the fridge, flinging the door open and grabbing random items. I take the lid off of the first bottle in my arsenal, whirl around, and start pitching it in his general direction. A-1 sauce rains down on his head and all over the kitchen floor.

His head jerks up as I empty the bottle and then toss it to the side, flipping up the lid on the squeeze-bottle of ketchup tucked under my arm before bringing it up above my head in both hands.

"You wouldn't."

"Oh, I would," I threaten before squeezing hard on the bottle. An arc of ketchup flies out and hits Gavin right in the chest.

He blinks at me in shock and then charges. Squealing, I throw the ketchup bottle to the ground and turn to run, but my foot slides right through a ketchup/A-1 mixture and I slip across the floor, landing right on my ass. Gavin jumps over me and opens the fridge, quickly turning around and dumping a jar of black olives and all the juice on top of my head.

"Eeew, eew, eew! Black olives are disgusting!" I screech.

"Yeah, how do you like it now, bitch!"

I stop screaming and glare up at him.

"Oops, my bad. Please don't kill me," he pleads.

"Gavin, you seriously need to get your mailing address changed. I'm getting tired of bringing over your—"

Uncle Carter stops at the doorway to the kitchen and looks back and forth between the two of us. I quickly pull the chef coat closed and avoid looking at him while I button it back up.

"Hey, Dad. So, what's new?" Gavin asks casually as he leans against the fridge.

Reaching over, I smack him in the leg and hold my hand out to him with an angry glare. He quickly grabs my hand and pulls me up off of the floor, moving me behind him so I'm not standing in front of his father, half-naked and covered in black olive juice.

"Well, at least you're not naked with Tyler again," Uncle Carter says with a sigh.

Gavin looks at me and whispers. "Don't ask."

Uncle Carter turns and walks out of the kitchen.

"Follow me," he shouts back to us.

Gavin and I stare at each other for a few minutes before he shrugs and grabs my hand, pulling me into the living room behind his dad. We find him sitting on the couch with his elbows on his knees and his hands clasped. I'm not going to lie, I'm a little freaked out right now. Uncle Carter is usually never this quiet. Is he going to yell at us? Be disappointed that we're kind of sort of together and haven't told the family?

"I was really afraid of this happening," Uncle Carter finally says with a sigh as we stand in front of him with our heads bowed like two kids at the principal's office.

Oh my God, here it comes. He's going to tell us what a bad

idea it is for us to be together. He knows Gavin doesn't love me and that it's only going to end in disaster.

Uncle Carter raises his head and looks back and forth between the two of us. "Be honest with me here. How long has this been going on?"

My heart is racing a mile a minute and I kind of want to cry. I can't believe this is happening.

"Um, like a week? Or something," Gavin mumbles.

"A week. Okay. Okay, we can fix this. That's not enough for any long-term damage," Uncle Carter says reassuringly.

Except I am NOT reassured. I am not reassured at all. What kind of long-term damage is he talking about? It's official. I'm going to have to marry my fake, gay boyfriend and spend the rest of my life never having awesome sex with the man I love ever again.

"I don't think we'll need hypnosis. Maybe just some mind-altering drugs. I wonder if acid would work. I've never done acid. It should be perfectly safe in small doses," Uncle Carter tells us.

"Dad, what the fuck are you talking about? I love Charlotte. We're not taking acid and nothing needs to be fixed," Gavin argues.

Wait, what the fuck?!

"I know you love her. Love has nothing to do with this," Uncle Carter complains.

I say again, THE FUCK?!

"Love has everything to do with it!" Gavin shouts.

"Gavin, I don't think you understand the seriousness of this situation. Look at the two of you. You're so young. It's not a path you want to go down."

"Dad, are you high right now? Seriously. Has Tyler been to your house? Did you eat any little pieces of chocolate he might have left behind?" Gavin demands.

"Gavin, listen to me. Whatever Uncle Drew and Aunt Jenny have taught you, there's still time for you to unlearn it. There's still hope for both of you to live normal, happy lives," Uncle Carter pleads.

"Dad, you are talking out of your ass right now. We are already living normal, happy lives." Gavin wraps his arm around my shoulder and pulls me in close to him. A black olive covered in ketchup drops out of my hair and lands on the ground by my feet with a *splat*.

Uncle Carter looks back and forth at us. "But you're covered in food. First it's food, then it's Skittles and a trip to the emergency room, and the next thing you know, you're out on the streets begging strangers for honey and jumper cables. JUST SAY NO to weird sex, GAVIN!"

Gavin starts to laugh and I probably would too if I wasn't in complete and utter shock at the words that came out of his mouth a few seconds ago.

"Dad, we have not been taking sex lessons from Uncle Drew and Aunt Jenny. Don't worry," Gavin reassures him.

Uncle Carter gets up from the couch and rushes toward us, wrapping his arms around both of us and squeezing us to him.

Just as quickly, he lets go of us and backs away toward the door.

"Well, alrighty then. You two kids have a nice evening."

Chapter 19

~ I Wanna Get the Craps ~

It's Halloween and my favorite holiday of the year. I should be a little more excited right now, but I'm not. Gavin and I still haven't discussed the bomb he dropped on me last week. Well, *I* haven't discussed it. I've done everything I can to avoid talking about it, including taking advice from Aunt Jenny.

"If you ever want to distract a guy from talking about something serious, just mention your period. It works every time. When Uncle Drew asks me if his butt looks big in a pair of jeans, I just tell him I've got cramps and he runs away screaming."

We've spent almost every day together and it's pretty obvious at this point that I'm not ready to talk about the whole "love" thing.

"So, don't you think we should talk about what happened at my place the other night?" Gavin asked.

"My ovaries feel like their being ripped out of my body right now, and I'm losing so much blood it could kill a horse, and you want to talk?!" I shouted in panic.

"I just ... I think my phone's ringing. At work. I'm going to get in my car and drive to work to answer my phone. The phone. At work," Gavin mumbled before turning and racing out of my house."

It's killing me not telling him I love him. But I have to figure out a way to get rid of my pretend gay boyfriend and still keep him as my friend without Gavin knowing what I've done. Piece of cake.

"Later."

"When later?"

"Just, later, alright?"

"But when? Isn't it time yet?"

"Jesus Christ, Drew, will you stop asking if it's time to go yet? We'll go when the pumpkins are finished being carved," Uncle Carter complains as I walk into Aunt Claire and Uncle Carter's kitchen.

Uncle Drew grumbles and flops down in one of the kitchen chairs.

Every year, we all go to a Halloween Walk in the Woods that the local Metro Park puts on. Uncle Carter always volunteers to carve a few pumpkins for their displays, and each year he tries to one-up the other volunteers on the level of pumpkin carving difficulty. This year, I think he's taken it to a whole new level.

"Sweetie, you should know by now to never tell Drew we're going somewhere. You just throw him in the car when it's time to leave," Aunt Claire reminds him as she comes into the kitchen. "Hey, Charlotte! Cute costume."

I look down at my knee high white socks, black four-inch Mary Jane's, short plaid skirt, and white button-down tied under my boobs, and I have to say, I'm pretty proud of myself. Rocco brought the outfit over earlier and helped me get dressed and even put my hair into pigtails.

"Where's Gavin?" I ask as I take in the scene in front of me. There are pumpkin guts everywhere, and Uncle Carter is so deep in concentration on carving the pumpkin in front of him that he doesn't even notice Uncle Drew has carved an extra piece of pumpkin into the shape of a penis and is currently pinning it to the back of Uncle Carter's pumpkin.

"Jenny's with him in the bathroom helping him finish up his costume. Oh my God, Carter. Who's going to get the pumpkin guts off of the ceiling?" Aunt Claire asks as she stares above the table.

"Don't worry, I'll scrape them off. It's my fault. The electric drill had a mind of its own," Uncle Carter replies as he starts gathering up all of the newspapers from the table with piles of guts on them.

"Is there any particular reason why you thought power tools were necessary when carving pumpkins? Our kitchen looks like Home Depot covered in shit right now," Aunt Claire complains as she looks around the room and sees a drill, a sander, an electric nail gun, a circular saw, and a soldering iron, along with enough extension cords to plug something in all the way to China. "Oh my God, there's pumpkin on the curtains."

"What's up, bitches and hos?!" Tyler shouts as he walks into the kitchen with a five-year-old little boy in tow.

"Yay, Tyler's here," Uncle Carter deadpans.

"Who's the kid?" Uncle Drew nods in the little boy's direction.

"This is my little cousin, Josh. Josh, say hi to everyone," Tyler tells him.

"This is stupid. I hate costumes," Josh complains as he tugs on the neck of his Batman cape.

"Tyler, your cousin's a dick, dude," Uncle Drew replies.

"I know. But my aunt and uncle are out of town and I got stuck babysitting him so-OWWW! SON OF A BITCH!" Tyler screams as Josh kicks him in the shin.

"You're a dick," Josh tells him.

"Never mind," Uncle Drew says. "Your cousin is awesome."

Gavin walks into the kitchen then and we both stare at each other with wide eyes. Word hasn't seemed to have spread through the family yet that we're sort of together so for right now, we decided to just try and act normal when we're with everyone. That's going to be impossible with the costume he's wearing right now and the way he's staring at mine.

"Is everyone ready to go? We should probably leave soon so we can get a good parking space," Gavin finally says, tearing his gaze away from me.

"Dude, what the fuck are you wearing?" Uncle Drew asks, getting up from his chair and walking over to Gavin.

"What?" Gavin asks in confusion, looking down at his costume and then back up at Uncle Drew.

"Seriously, that's what you're wearing? That's embarrassing."

"What's wrong with what he's wearing? He's a cowboy and I think he looks very handsome," Aunt Claire replies.

"He looks like that homo from Brokeback Mountain. I JUST CAN'T QUIT YOU! That movie was like ten years ago, Muppet fucker," Uncle Drew says with disappointment.

Gavin is wearing a barn coat with sheepskin lining over a button-down blue jean shirt, dark jeans, and cowboy boots. On his head is a black cowboy hat.

I want to shove him to the floor and fuck his brains out. Jesus, he looks good enough to eat.

"Who the hell are you supposed to be?" Gavin asks, pointing to Uncle Drew and his T-shirt that says: *Don't scare me, I poop easily.*

Uncle Drew reaches over to the kitchen table and grabs a mask, sliding it over his face. "I'm Michael Myers, bitch!"

"I don't think Michael Myers would wear a shirt like that," Uncle Carter tells him.

"Fuck all your mothers. Everybody poops, even Michael Myers. Is it later now? Can we finally go?"

"EEEEEEEEEEEEEEEEEEEEEEK!"

The scream echoes through the forest and makes us all wince at the ear-piercing sound as we walk along the dark trail through the trees.

We've been listening to these screams for the past twenty minutes as we make our way through the Halloween Walk. There are jack-o-lanterns with candles in them lining the walkway and helping us see where we were going, but other than that, it's pitch dark until we come up on another Halloween display every hundred yards or so.

Since it's dark, Gavin and I have been able to steal a few hand-holding moments here and there, and while everyone was occupied with one of the haunted houses, he pulled me around the side of the house, pressed me up against it, and kissed me in the dark. My legs are still a little bit shaky from that kiss.

We pass the tree of skeletons. Over two hundred glow-in-the-dark skeletons hang down from a tree that has black lights shining on it to make them seem even more eerie. A man dressed in all black with glow-in-the-dark bones on his clothes jumps out and yells, "Boo," which is the most recent cause for the ear-piercing scream.

"I swear to God if he screams one more time, I'm leaving his ass in the woods," Tyler complains.

"Be nice. This walk is a little more scary this year," I tell him.

"EEEEEEEEEEEEEEEEEEEEEEEK!"

I cringe as another shriek fills the night air and our small group trudges farther down the path.

"Seriously? You could see the mechanical arms on that thing," Tyler says with a roll of his eyes. "What a pussy."

I feel a tug on my hand and looked down at Josh, clutching tightly onto both Gavin and I as he walks between us.

"Hey, Charlotte. What the heck is wrong with the guy with the *poop* shirt? Why does he keep screaming so much?"

I laugh and shake my head at him.

"His name is Drew and he's a big baby, that's what's wrong with him," Gavin answers for me.

"Hey! I heard that," Uncle Drew yells from a few feet in front of us.

"You were supposed to hear that, dumbass," Gavin replies.

"Awwww, you said *ass*," Josh scolds.

"Yeah, so did you. So there!" Gavin sticks his tongue out at Josh.

We stop to look at a tombstone display while the others continue walking ahead.

"Are you ready to talk to me yet?" Gavin asks.

No! Distraction!

"Ha, look at that tombstone! It says *Bea A. Fraid*. Hilarious!" I say nervously.

"Charlotte, I lov—"

"MENSTRUAL CRAMPS!" I shout, cutting him off.

"What are men's tall craps?" Josh asks.

Shit, I forgot he's still with us.

"Do tall men get craps? I'm gonna be tall when I get bigger. I wanna get the craps," Josh adds. "Gavin, do you get the craps?"

Gavin looks down at Josh in horror and then back up at me. "I think I hear my mom calling us. WE'RE COMING, MOM!"

Gavin turns and walks away quickly, and I follow behind him with Josh.

"I'm gonna tell my mom I'm getting the craps. This is gonna be awesome!"

Well, at least kids are good for one thing.

Chapter 20

~ Old Man Balls ~

"EEEEEEEEEEEEEEEEEEEEEEK! SON OF A BITCH!"

We're almost finished with the walk when a man dressed up as the Grim Reaper is suddenly walking elbow-to-elbow with Uncle Drew, staring straight at him as he walks, not saying a word.

"Hey you! Mean guy! Get away from poop guy before he cries!" Josh yells.

We all laugh at the prospect of Uncle Drew breaking down in the middle of the woods crying, but Josh's shout stops the Grim Reaper in his tracks. He slinks back off into the woods to wait for the next group of unsuspecting walkers to come through so he can scare *them*.

There are a few more small houses set up along the path that they turned into haunted houses, and we come up to the first one. Aunt Claire didn't want to take Josh through it just in case it was too scary, but he insisted.

My dad bought him a light-up wand when we first got to the Halloween Walk, and he wields it in front of him as we slowly make our way into the house.

"Oh my God, oh my God, oh my God," Uncle Drew chants quietly over and over.

"Will you shut up?" Dad scolds him in a loud whisper.

Cobwebs hang from the ceiling, body parts with blood all over them litter the floor and dangle from the walls, and a strobe light flashes as the sounds of scary music is piped through the house. We twist and turn through the maze of the rooms, electronic bats falling down from the ceiling around one turn, a mummy popping up from a coffin around another, and a person dressed up like Freddy Kruger jumping out at us close to the exit.

As soon as the guy leaps out from behind the door and throws his razor fingernails up at us, Josh smacks him in the hand with his light stick.

"OW!" screams Freddy Kruger as he clutches his injured razor hand to his chest.

"Ha! Not so tough now, are you, Fred?" Uncle Drew laughs as he walks by the guy and out the exit.

"GAAAAAAAAAAAAAAAH!" Uncle Drew screams as the Grim Reaper guy steps out from the side of the house directly into his path. Uncle Drew holds his hands to his throat and starts choking on his own spit from yelling so loud.

"Drew, for God's sakes, keep it together, man," Dad mutters as I stick a finger in my ear in an attempt to rub out the ringing going on from Uncle Drew's girly screams.

"I pacifically told him he shouldn't go with us if he was going to be too scared," Aunt Jenny mutters. "Baby, do you need the Heineken Remover?" she asks as she walks over and starts smacking him on the back.

"I DON'T KNOW IF HE DOES, BUT I COULD SURE USE A HEINEKEN RIGHT NOW, JENNY!" Tyler shouts.

"Dude, why are you shouting?" Gavin asks.

"Didn't your aunt have like a stroke or something? Isn't that why she's a little off? I figure if I talk loudly she'll understand me," Tyler explains.

"No, no stroke. She's just kind of … special," Gavin adds nicely.

We continue down the path, following the lit jack-o-lanterns to the next haunted house. The Grim Reaper walks elbow to elbow with Uncle Drew the entire way, never once taking his eyes off of him.

"Okay, seriously, fucker. If you're going to follow me, at least say something. All this staring is wigging me out," Uncle Drew complains.

The man says nothing, just continues to keep pace with Uncle Drew. When he speeds up, the Grim Reaper speeds up. When he slows down, the Grim Reaper slows down. When he walks in a circle around our group as we stop to admire some of the carved pumpkins, the Grim Reaper follows right behind him.

At one point, Uncle Drew lifts his knee and holds his arms out to his side, touching his nose with each finger like he's doing a sobriety test. The Grim Reaper follows right along. Uncle Drew decides he's no longer just going to sit back and let this poor volunteer for the parks department get off easily. He hops like a rabbit for about two hundred yards and then sprints to the next haunted house.

The Reaper follows, mimicking his movements.

Eventually, Uncle Drew starts calling him Grimmy and invites the guy out for drinks after the walk but tells him he can only come along if he keeps the costume on.

Grimmy never answers.

I have to say, I've never seen a guy stay in character this well, especially with all the shit Uncle Drew is having him do. We go into a haunted house and the guy disappears into the woods. Then, a few minutes later, he's right back next to Uncle Drew, following him like a puppy dog.

And of course when we say something about that, Uncle Drew decides to crawl on all fours for a little while, barking every few feet.

Grimmy copies.

It takes about an hour to go through the entire Halloween Walk through the woods, so pretty soon, we're all kind of attached to Grimmy. When we walk over a small wooden bridge and look down into the water to see all of the jack-o-lanterns they place on pedestals in the water, Grimmy lifts Josh up so he can see over the railing.

When we come around a bend to see a graveyard setup on the hillside, Grimmy points out one of the big tombstones to Josh right before a ghost jumps out and tries to scare him. Josh walks right up to the ghost and kicks him in the shin.

If we could see Grimmy's face, I bet we would see him smile.

We come around the last corner of the walk and can see people milling about at the end getting hot chocolate and hot apple cider from some of the vendors.

Uncle Drew pats Grimmy on the back. "Well, Grimster, it's been fun. I'd say it was nice to meet you, but you scared the future children I might have had out of my nut sack when we first met."

"Future children? Your balls are too old to have any more kids," Dad laughs.

"I'll have you know that my sperm are in excellent condition and my balls are NOT old. I do NOT have old man balls. Honey, tell them." Uncle Drew looks over at Aunt Jenny.

"It's true. He doesn't have old man balls. They are still nice and soft and not wrinkly at all."

Grimmy puts his hand up over his masked eyes and shakes his head sadly.

We all wave at the guy as he stands in place in the middle of the path, and we make our way out of the woods. Gavin and I walk over to one of the stands, and he gets me some hot apple cider.

"I'm having a really hard time being with you tonight and not ripping every piece of clothing off of—"

"What are you kids talking about?" Aunt Claire asks as she comes up next to us.

"The weather."

"Astrophysics," Gavin and I reply at the same time.

Aunt Claire looks back and forth between us suspiciously.

"The direct correlation to the earth's atmosphere blending with the time space continuum to produce noxious gas on Mars," I ramble.

"Well, alright then. Have fun with that," she replies, turning around and walking back over the picnic table where everyone is seated.

"That was close. Nice save," Gavin says quietly with a laugh as we follow behind her.

"We need to be more careful or everyone's going to find out," I warn him as we walk.

"Who cares? You broke up with Rocco, right? So it doesn't matter."

ABORT! ABORT CONVERSATION!

"I think I need to change my tampon."

"Oh look, a squirrel!" Gavin says, rushing away from me and taking a seat next to Uncle Carter at the picnic table.

With a sigh, I take a seat across from him, next to Tyler and Josh. A man with a Metro Parks uniform walks up to our table and asks if we had a good time and enjoyed the walk.

"I beat up Freddy Kruger and kicked a ghost. It was alright," Josh replies with a shrug.

"I have to tell ya, man, that Grim Reaper you got walking around the woods deserves a raise. That guy scared the holy hell out of me," Uncle Drew tells him with a laugh.

We all chuckle and then notice the park worker looking at

Uncle Drew in confusion.

"Grim Reaper? We don't have a grim reaper employed with us this year, do you mean Frankenstein?" he asks.

"Uh, no. I mean the Grim Reaper. Tall guy, wearing a black cloak that dragged on the ground and had a hood pulled around his face so you couldn't see him. And he had that big sickle thing in his hand that he walked with," Uncle Drew explains.

"I'm sorry, sir, there is definitely no one of that description that works here this year."

We all look around at one another in confusion, no one wanting to admit just how creeped out we are. But I know there has to be a logical explanation.

"It was probably just someone going on the walk like we were and he decided to have some fun with you," I tell Uncle Drew.

Once again, the park worker shakes his head.

"I was at the front gate collecting tickets from everyone tonight, and there wasn't anyone wearing a costume like that," he says.

The man talks to us for a few more minutes about the people that volunteer for the walk every year and how he's known them since the walk first opened twenty years ago. He walks away and our table stays silent while everyone processes what he'd said.

"Maybe he was a homeless guy or something. I bet he lives in the woods and just wanted to make some friends," Aunt Jenny says wistfully.

"Make some friends, yeah right. That guy wanted to ass rape me," Uncle Drew complains.

"Really, Drew? I'm surprised you noticed anything while you were humping trees and squatting over pumpkins so it looked like you were shitting them out." Mom gets a disgusted look on her face as she remembers Uncle Drew's actions in the woods.

"Oh believe me, I could tell. There was something squirrely about him," Uncle Drew says with a nod of his head.

"Wait a minute. You thought he was a squirrel? I thought he was supposed to be the Grim Reaper?" Aunt Jenny says in confusion.

Uncle Drew pats her hand. "No, baby. It's just a figure of … never mind."

"I still say he's homeless. It's a doggy-dog world out there. Poor guy was probably just trying to make some money," Aunt Jenny adds.

Tyler looks at her in confusion. "Don't you mean *dog eat dog* world?"

"Jenny lives in the puppies and rainbows part of the globe," Aunt Claire says with a laugh.

"Is there really a place like that?" Aunt Jenny asks.

"He told me what his name was," Josh says nonchalantly.

Uncle Drew looks across the table at Josh. "Dude, shut up. No he didn't."

"YOU shut up. He totally did," Josh argues, looking over his shoulder, back into the woods with a nervous look taking over his face.

We all turn our heads and stare in silence toward the trail entrance.

"What did he tell you his name was?" Aunt Claire asks quietly.

Everyone leans closer to Josh, no one saying a word, waiting for him to speak.

"He said …"

Everyone holds their breath.

"His name …"

No one blinks.

"Was …"

My heart is beating out of my fucking chest and my knee is bouncing nervously under the table. I feel Gavin's hand reach under the table and clutch my knee.

"Death," Josh whispers seriously.

We all sit there staring at Josh with our mouths dropped, the silence permeating the air around us.

"Holy shit," Uncle Drew whispers.

"I'm going to find security and tell them," Dad says as he starts to get up from the bench.

"I'll come with you," Uncle Carter states, doing the same.

Josh scrambles off of the picnic table bench and starts laughing hysterically. "You guys are a bunch of sissies! He said his name is Bob and he was opposed to be dressed like a ghost but he got hot chocolate all over his costume and had to change!"

Everyone lets out the breaths they'd been holding as Josh continues to laugh and taunt everyone.

"Oh my God, we just got punked by a five-year-old," Uncle Drew says with admiration in his voice.

Well, after this fun-filled evening, telling Gavin about Rocco should be no big deal.

Chapter 21

~ Run Virginityman! ~

"So, the plan is you're going to just break up with me in front of Gavin? I don't know if I like this," Rocco complains as he stands in my living room.

"You will do it and you will like it, or I will never go shoe shopping with you ever again!" I threaten.

Rocco places his hand over his heart and pouts. "Now that's just mean."

I am such a chickenshit. I should have told him when we got back to his apartment after the Halloween walk last night. Instead, I dragged him into the shower and gave him a blow job. Blow jobs equal love, right?

My mom invited a few people over for dinner, so I figure this is the perfect time for a public break-up. I can just end things with Rocco, pretend like the list never happened, and we can all move on.

"Charlotte, your mom needs help in the kitchen," my dad says as he walks into the living room. He stops when he sees Rocco and glares at him.

"Oh, no worries, Dad. I'd be glad to help Liz in the kitchen. I could even whip up a soufflé if there's time," Rocco tells him.

"Seriously, dial down the gay a notch," I whisper.

"I mean, how 'bout we grab us a few brewskies and see if there's a fight on TV," Rocco tells my dad in a deep voice.

"How about I give you a five second head start before I get my shotgun," he replies.

"LIZ! Get your ass out here and help me carry these cupcakes," Aunt Claire yells as she walks through the front door. "Oh … hi, guys. Jim, stop staring at that poor boy like you want to slit his throat. LIZ!"

Mom comes rushing into the living room, wiping her hands on a towel. "What the fuck is your problem? Stop shouting already. Rocco, when did you get here? What are you doing here? Why is he here?"

"I really think your family is going to be crushed when you break my heart," Rocco whispers in my ear.

The front door opens again and in walk Uncle Carter and Gavin, both of them smiling and laughing until they see Rocco standing next to me.

Shit. Maybe this wasn't the best idea.

Rocco moves to stand behind me and clutches onto the back of my shirt. "Don't let them hit me! I just had a facial!" he whispers frantically.

"What's he doing here?" Gavin demands.

"Want to go help me clean my gun?" Dad asks him.

Aunt Claire smacks my dad on the arm.

Oh my God, Gavin looks pissed. He has every right to look pissed. I kind of sort of alluded to the fact that I was breaking up with Rocco a few weeks ago and haven't mentioned him once since Gavin and I started fooling around. This is bad. Very bad.

I quickly turn around to face Rocco. "Rocco, I'm breaking up with you."

"WHAT?! NOOOOOOOO!" Rocco screams. "Baby, please don't leave me!"

I widen my eyes at him and scowl. "Nope. It's over. I don't love you. I've never loved you. You should just go now."

"OH MY GOD MY LIFE IS OVER!" Rocco wails, throwing his arms around me and sobbing into my shoulder.

"OVER. ACTING," I say through clenched teeth.

He quickly pulls back and puffs out his chest. "Whatev, babe. It's cool."

With that, he walks around me and heads to the door, passing Ava as she comes in with Tyler.

"Oooooh, cute shoes!" Rocco says before walking out, the door slamming closed behind him.

"So, who's hungry? I'm starving!" I announce to the room as they all stand there staring at me.

"Hey, Charlotte, what's with this list I found on your desk?" Molly asks, walking into the room from the back hallway. "Show him your cleavage, make him change your tire, have him lick chocolate off of you …"

Molly trails off when she finally looks up and sees me staring at her in horror. Gavin walks past me and right up to Molly, snatching the piece of paper out of her hands reading through it. As his eyes widen in what I assume to be horror while he scans the list, I seriously contemplate turning and running out of the house. Maybe leaving the country and changing my name.

"Gavin, I can explain," I tell him softly, trying not to cry.

Gavin doesn't say anything as he continues reading.

Tyler walks across the room and glances over Gavin's shoulder. "Ooooh, that's a good one. *Take him to a sporting event and act like you know what's going on.* He would have totally fallen for that."

Gavin puts his hand over his mouth, and I'm wondering if it's going to be the mustard episode all over again and he's going to start gagging. I see his shoulders start to shake and suddenly realize he's laughing. He's fucking laughing at my list.

"What the hell is so funny?" I demand.

I don't care if I'm in the wrong here. He's laughing at my misguided attempt to get him to fall in love with me. It's really not a laughing matter.

Gavin moves his hand away and laughs out loud. "Tyler, I think you should tell her what's so funny."

"Holy fuck, it's about time," Tyler complains, reaching into his back pocket and pulling out a folded up piece of notebook paper, handing it over to me.

I stare at it in confusion for a few seconds before Gavin speaks through his laughs. "You really need to open that."

With a sigh, I unfold the paper and scan the words written in Tyler's messy handwriting. I really don't need to read everything; the title at the top of the page pretty much says it all.

"Oh my God," I mutter.

Gavin comes up to me and places both of his hands on my cheeks, pulling my head up so he can look into my eyes. "I'm not crazy, right? This means you love me?"

I laugh and shake my head at him. "You idiot. Of course I love you. I loved you even when you were mutilating my Barbies and calling me a labia. I'm pretty sure giving you my virginity should have been clue number one."

Too late, I realize we're not alone in this room.

"Gavin, I love you like a son, but right now I want to punch you in your face," Dad tells him.

"Can you wait to kick my ass until after I kiss your daughter, please?" Gavin begs him.

"Fine. You've got ten seconds. And then I'm ripping off your dick and giving you your own labia," Dad threatens, crossing his arms over his chest.

Gavin doesn't waste any of those ten seconds. He swoops down and presses his lips to mine.

"Oh my God, I'm totally going to cry. Liz, get me a tissue," Aunt Claire says.

"Get your own fucking tissue, you whore," Mom sniffles.

"I'm still wearing the blue dress to the wedding," Aunt Claire tells her as I wrap my arms around Carter's neck.

"We are going to throw down right the fuck now. Jim, get the *Fight Club* DVD. This is totally happening," Mom states.

"I'm going to punch you right in the ovaries."

"Yeah, well I'm going to be the first one to walk down the aisle, so you're going to look like a dick when you waltz down in your subpar blue dress."

"I'm going to make you wear a suck-for-a-buck shirt at her bachelorette party."

"Oh no you DIDN'T just say that to me!"

"Oh yeah, that JUST happened!"

"Their first born is going to be named after me."

"Your name is bullshit."

"YOU'RE BULLSHIT!"

Breaking the kiss, I pull back and look at Gavin.

"Are you sure about this? I don't know if our families are going to survive," I tell him softly with a smile.

"Jim, get me the basket of dinner rolls from the kitchen. There are twelve with Claire's face written all over them."

"Carter, get me the mashed potatoes and turn on the ceiling fan. This bitch is going down."

Gavin laughs and shakes his head. "Love and lists. Just remember, love and lists. Nothing else matters."

Pulling Gavin's mouth back down to mine, I forget all about the chaos surrounding us and just enjoy the moment.

"Alright, that's enough. Break it up. I've got a face to beat up," my dad announces.

Gavin looks over my shoulder and his smile instantly falls. "Oh shit. He's serious."

"Run, Virginityman, run!" Tyler shouts.

Epilogue

- Gavin -

Hand in hand with Charlotte, we walk around to the back of her parents' house. It's no longer her house anymore since she moved into my apartment last week.

Can I get a round of applause, folks?! Or maybe just a "FUCK YEAH!"?

"This is so weird. Just a few months ago I was making this same walk with Tyler, giving myself a pep talk about my list," I tell Charlotte with a laugh.

"Yeah, well I was inside the house at that same time freaking out about whether or not Rocco was going to be convincing as my boyfriend," she replies.

"I'm so glad I never killed him. He has great taste in shoes." I look down at her platform wedges that make her long legs look fucking hot.

"Don't even think about it, Gavin. We are not sneaking off into the bushes to have sex at my parents' house," Charlotte warns me as I continue to stare at her legs while we walk.

"That's probably a wise decision since I'm pretty sure my puke is still in those bushes."

Once Charlotte finally came clean that she and Rocco were never really dating, he and I actually became good friends. I've had to put him in his place a few times when he makes comments about my great ass, but all in all, having a gay dude as a friend is pretty awesome. I pretend like I never hated him or wished that a rabid infestation of crabs would chew off his dick, and he takes me shopping to pick out sexy shoes and lingerie for Charlotte. It's perfect.

I'm still working my ass off at Seduction and Snacks and loving every minute of it, especially now that I have a new co-worker. Charlotte accepted a position as the new Media Sales Rep for the business, and Aunt Liz couldn't be happier. We all decided that from now on it would be a good idea for *her* to do the ribbon cutting ceremonies at sex toy shops. Less chance of humiliating newspaper headlines that way since I'm pretty sure Charlotte won't be ODing on Viagra anytime soon. At least I hope not. I wonder what Viagra does to a vagina? I should ask Uncle Drew. I'm sure he knows.

As soon as we get to the back yard, we're immediately greeted by the sounds of screaming.

"GAAAAAAAAAAAAAAAAAAAAAAAH!"

"What the fuck is that?" I ask Uncle Drew as he walks

up to us.

"That, my little asshole, is a screaming goat. Molly showed me this awesome video on YouTube and I had to get one," Uncle Drew says with a huge smile.

"GAAAAAAAAAAAAAAAAAAAAAAH!"

Uncle Drew turns around and points proudly to a little black and white goat tied to one of Aunt Liz and Uncle Jim's trees. "Isn't she cute? Her name is Taylor Swift."

"GAAAAAAAAAAAAAAAAAAAAAAAH!" the goat screams as she looks right at us.

"I don't even understand what is happening right now," I reply with a shake of my head.

"I've been trying to teach her—"

"GAAAAAAAAAAAAAAAAAAAAAAH!"

"How to sing a—"

"GAAAAAAAAAAAAAAAAAAAAAAH!"

"Song, but she never comes in at the right—"

"GAAAAAAAAAAAAAAAAAAAAAAH!"

"SON OF A BITCH, TAYLOR SWIFT! I TOLD YOU, NOT UNTIL THE CHORUS!" Uncle Drew yells across the yard as he turns and walks away from us.

"Do you think Uncle Drew is ever going to grow up?" Charlotte asks me as we watch him have a conversation with the goat, his arms flying in every direction as he tries to explain to her what she did wrong.

"Definitely not."

I turn toward Charlotte and wrap my arms around her waist. I start to lean down for a kiss, but of course we're interrupted.

"You two need to get a room. All of this PDA shit is disgusting."

Charlotte and I turn our heads as Ava walks up next to us, with Tyler right behind her.

"Oh, don't be jealous, sugar muffin. Some day you'll be able to save up enough money and pay a guy off to love you that much," Tyler says with a smirk.

"Hey, Tyler, want to know what it feels like to have a stiletto shoved up your ass?" Ava casually asks him while she examines her fingernails.

"You already had your finger in my ass, so I'm assuming it wouldn't be much different."

Ava continues to stare at the chipped polish on her thumbnail, but I can tell she's about ready to lose it. Her nostrils flare and she lets out a growl.

"Dude, you might want to start running now," I whisper to him.

Unfortunately for Tyler, Ava isn't about to make a scene in her parents' backyard by beating the shit out of him. She's going for complete and total mind fuck right now.

"Remember the last time you were in my car and you left that My Little Pony toy in the center console?" Charlotte asks him sweetly, finally looking up at him.

Tyler loses all of his smugness and his smile falters.

"You didn't," he whispers.

"Know what happens when you put My Little Pony in the

microwave?" Ava asks.

Tyler's eyes widen and he clenches his fists at his sides. "No. Please, not Twilight Sparkle."

Ava takes a few steps in his direction until she's right up in his face. "She put up a good fight. She screamed until the bitter end."

Tyler grits his teeth and if I'm not mistaken, I think I see a few tears pooling in his eyes. He's quiet for so long that I wonder if maybe he's going to take the high road and just walk away. Too bad Ava sticks the knife in a little deeper by smiling brightly at him. That's all it takes to push Tyler over the edge.

"YOU CRAB INFESTED CROTCH ROT! I was lying about those jeans the other day. They TOTALLY make your ass look fat!"

"YOU FUCKER! Did you just call me a fat-ass? YOU HAVE A SMALL PENIS!" Ava yells.

"I don't have a small penis. Your vagina is just bigger than the fucking Grand Canyon!"

"I HATE YOU!" Ava screams.

"I HATE YOU MORE!" Tyler adds.

They both stand nose-to-nose, chests heaving and staring angrily at one another. I start to pull away from Charlotte to break up the fight when Tyler suddenly speaks.

"You're so fucking hot. Your car or mine?"

"Mine. I parked closer."

Ava grabs Tyler's hand and drags him across the yard to the driveway.

"Those two are going to kill each other." Charlotte sighs with a shake of her head as we watch them hustle away.

"At least they're going to maim each other in *her* car. Tyler borrowed mine today, remember? I don't think I can get severed head stains out of the upholstery."

Now that we're alone again, I turn back toward Charlotte and pull her close. There's nothing better than being able to touch her and hold her whenever I want. Except for having sex with her. Having sex with her is definitely better.

Taking up where we left off before the tornado of Tyler and Ava came screaming through the yard, I lean my head down to Charlotte for a kiss. She quickly brings her hand up in front of my face to stop me.

"I know this whole thing is still kind of new with us, but I feel like I should tell you something really important. It might have a huge impact on our relationship," she tells me softly.

"As long as you don't tell me you have another fake, gay boyfriend somewhere, nothing else matters," I laugh.

"No. Rocco is the only fake, gay boyfriend I will ever have. You can count on that."

Charlotte takes a deep breath and spits it out. "The thing is, I never want to have children. I really like my vagina, and I'm pretty sure you do too. I have no desire to push a tiny little human out of it and destroy the poor thing forever."

I stare at her in silence for a few seconds before one corner of my mouth turns up in a grin.

Fuck, do I love this girl.

"Good. Because I can't stand kids. And the thought of your

vagina turning into something that looks like finely sliced roast beef is not appealing to me at all."

"Eeeew, that's disgusting," Charlotte replies, scrunching her nose up.

"Sorry, I heard my mom say that once and it's always stuck with me," I tell her.

Charlotte wraps her arms around my neck and stands up on her tiptoes. "Well, it's a good thing your mom never felt like that about kids or you wouldn't be here with me right now."

I hear someone clear her throat and turn to see my mom standing next to us with a sheepish look on her face. "Yeah, about that ..."

- The End -

**Turn the page for an exciting excerpt
from Madeline Sheehan's novel**

UNBEAUTIFULLY

(Undeniable #2)
Danny & Ripper's Story!

UnBeautifully

(Undeniable #2)

Danny & Ripper's Story

by

Madeline Sheehan

"No sooner met but they looked,

no sooner looked but they loved,

no sooner loved but they sighed,

no sooner sighed but they

asked one another the reason,

no sooner knew the reason

but they sought the remedy ..."

—William Shakespeare

PROLOGUE

I don't believe in fate. I firmly believe that life is what you make of it, that life will react to your actions, and that your final destination has nothing to do with destiny but instead everything to do with the choices you make along the way.

With one exception.

Love.

There are no rules when it comes to love.

Love is not a reaction or an action; it is not a destiny or a choice.

Love is a feeling, a real, raw, and unscripted emotion so sensationally pure, unable to dull even under the strain of a world against it, strong enough to heal the broken and warm even the coldest of hearts.

Innate.

Unavoidable.

Undeniable.

And sometimes, love is unconventional and it breaks all the rules and blurs all the lines and basks in its glory, shining as bright as the sun, unapologetically glowing even under the narrowed stares of society and its screaming, self-righteous morals, berating and judging that which it doesn't understand.

The first time I fell in love, it was with a pair of blue eyes and a wide, dimpled grin.

"Your old man loves ya, Danny girl," he whispered. "You never, ever forget that, yeah?"

I never did. And I never thought I could ever love any man as much as I loved my father. But as we grow, we change, we begin to make our own decisions and thus become independent and self-sufficient, and start turning away from our parents and turning to others. We begin experiencing life outside of the bubble we grew up in and form friendships, strong bonds, and unbreakable ties.

And we fall in love … a second time.

The second time I fell in love it was with a badly scarred face, the stuff of nightmares, the sort of disfigurement that mothers steer their children away from. Ugly, jagged slashes marred the skin from the top of his skull, down over his right eye, an eye that had been dug out of his face with a serrated blade. The scars continued across his cheek, over his lips, and down his neck, ending at the top of his shoulder. His chest was a hundred times worse, scar tissue as far as the eye could see.

"Baby," he said gruffly. "Man like me got no business with a girl like you. You're nothin' but fuckin' beauty and I'm a whole lot of fuckin' ugly who's already halfway to hell."

But he was wrong.

Everything has beauty. Even the ugly. Especially the ugly.

Because without ugly, there would be no beauty.

Because without beauty, we would not survive our pain, our sorrow, and our suffering.

And in the world I lived in, the world he lived in, a secret world within the world, a world of constant crime and cruelty, a cold world full of despair and death, there was almost nothing but suffering.

"You may not be beautiful the way you were before," I whispered, cupping his ruined cheek. "But you're still beautiful. To me."

Ours was the furthest thing from a picture-perfect romance; it was more of a car crash, a metal-bending, blood-splattered disaster that left no survivors, only bad memories and heartache.

But it was ours.

And because it was ours … I wouldn't change a thing.

Chapter One

Slipping on a pair of sunglasses, I stepped out of the clubhouse into the bright midday Montana sun and surveyed the backyard where my family, both related by blood and not, were enjoying a Saturday afternoon cookout. If the sun was shining and the weather decent, this was how the Miles City, Montana, chapter of the Hell's Horsemen Motorcycle Club, or MC, unwound.

The voices of Willie Nelson, Waylon Jennings, Johnny Cash and Kris Kristofferson were belting the lyrics of "Highwayman" through the speakers, the sizzling scents of cooking meat floated tantalizingly along the warm breeze, and children were running back and forth playing with inflatable beach balls and water guns.

My father, Deuce, the Horsemen's president, stood off to the side of the party, drinking beer with his father-in-law, Damon "Preacher" Fox, president of the notorious Silver Demons Motorcycle Club run out of New York City. Across the yard, my stepmother Eva, her friends Kami and Dorothy, and a few bikers and their old ladies were deep in conversation.

I headed for my father.

"Hey, darlin'," he said, swinging a thick, heavy arm across my

Tara Sivec

shoulders and pulling me into a hug, crushing my face against his leather cut, the vest worn from age and use.

The scent of bike fumes, sweat-stained leather, and cigarette smoke filled my nostrils and I inhaled deeply. I loved that smell. It was the smell of my childhood, the smell of safety and home.

My very first memory was of being three years old, metal and Harley Davidson wings gleaming in the sunlight, the thick, acrid smell of exhaust fumes, clouds of cigarette smoke, stale sweat stained yellow on white T-shirts, the bitter sting of alcohol filling my nostrils, worn and cracked leather soft against my cheek, grease-stained hands lifting me up into the air, accompanied by loud, raucous laughter.

I smiled up at my father. "Love you, Daddy."

Grinning, he planted a big, wet kiss on my forehead.

Even at fifty-three, my father was a great-looking guy. He was tall and broad, thickly muscled, with a pair of sparkling ice blue eyes identical to my own. His graying hair was long and blond, usually pulled back, and a short beard framed his face. But it was his grin that got him into trouble. My father grinned and women swooned.

Honestly, I didn't have a clue how Eva put up with all the female attention he got around the club. Whenever I asked, she'd always shrug and say, "It's typical."

Eva and I were both biker brats, but whereas Preacher raised her inside his clubhouse alongside his boys, I was raised at home. I frequented the clubhouse on occasion but hadn't become an integral part of "the life" until my father brought Eva home with

232

him, pregnant with my little sister, Ivy, about five years back. And everything changed.

Because of Eva, I'd been able to start spending more time at the club, *finally getting a chance to know the men I'd known all my life but had never gotten the chance to really, truly know until now. I'd formed relationships with all of them—Tap, Bucket, ZZ, Marsh, Hawk, Mick, Freebird, Cox, Blue, Chip, Worm, Dimebag, Dirty, and Jase. And also Danny D. and Danny L. who, because they had the same first name as me, I ended up calling them DoubleD and DL, which they loved, and eventually the names stuck.*

They were all so different, young and old, their appearances varying as much as their ages, but they all had one thing in common.

Brotherhood.

It was everything to them; they would take a bullet for one another as soon as take their next breath. And my father, their president, in return for their loyalty took care of them and their families. It was a never-ending cycle of allegiance and respect and ... love.

Even so, I knew this life wasn't all sunshine and roses. Being the daughter of a hardened criminal, I knew sunshine and roses for what they really were. Few and far between. Especially in my family.

When I was seven my father attended a parent/teacher conference with my mother. It was his first and his last. My second grade teacher had made the mistake of informing my parents I was falling behind in class and would probably need to repeat second grade. Needless to say, my father took this as a slam against me and a personal insult to his parenting. Mr. Steinberg never did return to teaching after he'd recovered from his injuries.

When I was twelve my brother took on four boys who were picking on me and in turn got his ass kicked. As he limped away, he spit out a tooth and grinned at me. "They'll think twice next time, little sister," he said, slinging his arm over my shoulders. "No one's gonna mess with a girl who's got a brother crazy enough to take on four guys at once."

And I thought ... that's what love is.

To some, the idea of violence being interpreted as love is ludicrous, but to me, it was my reality. It is my reality.

"Hiya, Danny girl," Preacher said, holding out his arms.

My father let me go and I wrapped my arms around Preacher's middle and squeezed.

"Lookin' gorgeous as always, sweetheart," he said in his gruff, raspy voice. He gave me a quick kiss on the cheek and released me.

Grabbing a beer from a cooler, I crossed the lawn headed for Eva. Talking with Kami, Eva paused to shoot me a quick smile. Eva and Kami were polar opposites in every way. Married with two kids with Cox, my father's super sexy tattooed and pierced road chief, Kami was blue-eyed and blonde, tall and runway-model thin, whereas Eva had smoky gray eyes, long dark hair, and curves. But they were kindred spirits, had been friends for thirty years now, and I often found myself jealous of what they shared, their ability to tell each other anything and everything, to be there for each other no matter what.

I'd never had that. With anyone.

And I wanted it. Desperately.

But I've wanted a lot of things over the years that I'd never gotten, and eventually I learned to accept the fact that some things would forever be out of my reach.

I stepped up beside Dorothy, placed my palm on her swollen belly, and gave her a light rub. Blowing out a breath, she shoved her red hair out of her eyes and covered my hand with hers.

"Only a few more weeks, Danny." She sighed. "I can't wait for this baby to come out. I'm too old to be pregnant."

I gave her a sympathetic smile.

At thirty-six, Dorothy wasn't old, but she was an old soul. She'd gotten pregnant at sixteen, married at eighteen, and had lived for too long in a bad marriage with a man who wanted nothing to do with her. In her early twenties she met Jase, one of my father's lifers and, and started coming to the club to be with him when he wasn't at home with his wife, Chrissy, and their three kids.

Dorothy Kelley wasn't like the rest of the club whores that flocked to the MC. She truly loved Jase and Jase adored her. Just not enough to leave his wife. Now she was a permanent fixture at the club. She was paid to cook, clean, and do the laundry, and she'd since left her husband and lived in an apartment Jase paid for in town. Her daughter, Tegen, two years younger than me, was away at college in San Francisco. Now, Dorothy spent practically all of her time at the club. She and I had grown close over the past four years, and although I disapproved of the love triangle she was involved in, I loved her with all my heart.

A familiar arm slid around my middle and pulled me close.

"Hey, baby," ZZ whispered, slipping his fingertips in the waistband of my jeans. With his other hand, he grabbed my beer and took a long swallow.

I turned into his big, hard body and slipped my arms around his waist. "Hey, you," I whispered back, kissing his sternum.

ZZ was another lifer, thirty years old, big and strong, long brown hair, matching brown eyes, squared handsome features, and a perpetual five o'clock shadow. And he was a sweetheart. As far as boyfriends went, I'd hit the jackpot. Kind and thoughtful, educated and well-read, faithful in a club constantly filled with whores, ZZ was everything a girl could hope for in a man.

"Evie." Kami laughed. "Big, sexy, and scary is staring again."

We all turned to find my father watching Eva the way he always watched Eva. Intense. Wholly possessive. Sexual to the nth degree.

Grossed out, I turned away.

"Watch this," Eva whispered, and bent over to pick up Kami's one-year-old son, Diesel. Her jeans pulled down, her shirt pulled up, and deuce, tattooed above her ass in large scrolling script, was front and center in my father's line of sight.

I didn't have to look to know my father was ten seconds away from stalking across the lawn and throwing her over his shoulder. That he was a caveman, when it came to Eva, was putting it mildly. As happy as I was that they were happy, the ick factor at watching my father always groping my stepmother was off the charts.

But all that said, my father and Eva had come a long way. A few years back, right before my eighteenth birthday, Eva's now deceased husband, Frankie "Crazy" Deluva, had brutalized her in front of my father. The whole ordeal had ended with Eva forced to kill her husband, all of which had left her relationship with my father terribly damaged. It had been a hard road back, and seeing them like this, happy and still very much in love, was truly a blessing.

"You're terrible," Adriana scolded Eva, laughing.

Adriana's husband, Mick, my father's VP and best friend, pulled her close and kissed her cheek.

"Babe," he growled. "I'm thinkin' you need to start bein' more terrible."

Adriana giggled.

"Be right back, babe," ZZ whispered, kissing my lips as he squeezed my backside. Grabbing Mick, he flashed me a shit-eating grin and took off across the lawn just as a blaze of pink and pigtails came streaking by.

"Get back here, you crazy little shit!" Cage bellowed, running after Ivy. "And give me my keys!"

Laughing like a maniac, Ivy kept running. Cage ran faster, shooting past her, and Ivy tried to go left, but Cage was quicker and grabbed her.

"Gotcha!" he said as she shrieked and giggled until he set her down.

"Ivy Olivia West!" Eva yelled. "Give your brother his keys!"

"Here," Ivy muttered, slapping the keys into his outstretched hand. Cage's hand closed around hers and he pulled her forward into a bear hug.

"Love you, you crazy little shit," he growled. "Couldn't have asked for a better sister. 'Cause, ya know, Danny's kinda bitchy."

Rolling my eyes, I flipped them off and in return received two grins identical to my own.

I shook my head. Ivy was learning all of her life lessons from our arrogant, womanizing, prankster of a brother. The arrogance I couldn't fault him for. He was a great-looking guy, a younger, less harsh version of our father. Tall and muscular with long blond hair and dark chocolate eyes, the girls loved him. And he loved them back. However, the womanizing and constant pranks I could fault him for, and Ivy was following in his footsteps. She knew just the right thing to say to get her way, putting on the perfect pouty face and batting her wide blue eyes … ugh. And Eva, always keeping her in pigtails and Chucks, making both my father's and brother's hearts melt every time they laid eyes on her. Blech. Blargh. Blah. I had no doubt when she was older, she would be giving our elderly father several dozen heart attacks.

"She is such a little monster," Eva said, smiling fondly at Ivy.

"An adorable monster," Kami added.

"Ha," Eva scoffed. "You only think she's adorable because you don't h—"

Done with the conversation, I shoved my hands in my pockets and walked off, weaving my way through the groups of bikers, women, and children who were talking, laughing, dancing. It was serene. Picture-perfect.

Well, almost picture-perfect.

"Danny!"

Cringing, I spun around ready to hurry in the opposite direction but wasn't fast enough. My longtime friend Anabeth snatched my bicep and yanked me sideways. I stumbled to a stop and faced her. Like me, Anabeth was blonde, blue-eyed, and pretty. We were both in shape but whereas Anabeth was thin, I was more muscular. Ten years of gymnastics and four years of cheerleading will do that to you. I kept my hair long, highlighted, and styled, and Anabeth had hers short, cut into a smooth bob with razor-straight bangs. Currently she was wearing a deep blue mini dress and chunky blue espadrilles. In her ears were giant blue hoops, much like the fifty-plus she had on each of her arms. A few years ago I would have complimented her outfit, would have been wearing something similar myself, most likely pink. But that wasn't the case anymore. Anabeth and I were worlds apart. Actually, everyone and I were worlds apart ...

I'd lost something inside of me, something important, something special that had made me who I'd been, and slowly the color had seeped out of my world.

Anabeth gave my dark-washed jeans and black V-neck tee a once-over. Her gaze landed on my feet and she narrowed her eyes. "Are you wearing green ... Converse sneakers?"

Sighing, I looked down at my feet. I was. Chucks were all Eva wore aside from a few pairs of flip-flops, so in turn, Chucks were all Ivy and I got when Eva went shoe shopping. Combined, I would say the three of us had about a hundred pairs in a wide variety of colors.

"I kinda like them," I said and shrugged.

"I dig 'em," Freebird said. Freebird was an old biker who'd left his brain back in nineteen sixty-five. He had his old lady with him today, Apple Dumplin', who, like him, had long gray hair and more wrinkles then a crinkled-up piece of paper.

"Wat up, Danny girl?" Tap said, holding out his fist. I fist-bumped him and smiled.

Tap was in his late forties, not overly tall but made up for what he lacked in height in muscle. Built like a boxer, his muscles along with his long black hair and goatee were intimidating unless you knew him. He was one of the Horsemen's most even-tempered boys.

"Hannah says her hellos. She's hopin' you're comin' to visit Atlanta again soon."

Hannah was Tap's daughter. When Tap's wife, Tara, had left him, she'd taken Hannah and moved to Atlanta. Hannah was older than me, but we were both the daughters of Horsemen and had always known each other.

"I called her last week," I said, smiling. "She told me the good news."

He grinned. "Can't believe my baby's havin' a baby."

"Here ya go, babe," Ripper said, shoving in between Tap and Apple, offering a bottle of beer to Anabeth.

"Thanks," Anabeth said, smiling up at him.

Ripper stared down at Anabeth, his lips curving into a grin, his expression smug, knowing.

My stomach lurched and I quickly turned away, wanting to make a hasty exit before he noticed I was standing there. Ripper and I were … There just weren't words for what Ripper and I were.

I was three years old when my father met Erik "Ripper" Jacobs at a bike rally while on a run through San Antonio. Ripper was only seventeen at the time, having just lost both his parents to a drunk driving accident back home in Los Angeles. He had skipped town two days after the funeral on a stolen motorcycle, just three weeks before his high school graduation.

The boys liked him immediately, and when the Hell's Horsemen returned to Montana, he was with them.

After only three months of doing grunt work around the club, he was unanimously voted and patched in as a brother. A year later, my father promoted him to sergeant at arms and coined him "Ripper" after "Jack the Ripper," for being as talented with a blade as he was.

Being so young and new to the club and the life, moving up in the ranks so quickly was virtually unheard of. But Ripper was special and everyone knew it. He always had a smile on his face, a joke on the tip of his tongue. He was good with people, could talk nearly anyone into anything just by flashing a grin.

"Hey there, Ripper!" Apple said happily. "Danny was just tellin' us that she talked to Hannah last week. Tell us what else she said, Danny girl."

I stopped retreating and turned slowly back around. Ripper's deep blue gaze found mine.

He had his glass eye in today, a very realistic copy of the one that had been painfully taken from him, along with his fun-loving personality, by the same man who'd almost ruined my father's relationship with Eva. Frankie.

But Ripper didn't care about how he looked, unless …

I glanced back at Anabeth.

Unless he was trying to impress someone.

I pushed my sunglasses up over my head. "Ripper," I greeted him evenly.

We stared at each other.

Whore, I thought bitterly.

His expression went cold. Don't start, Danny, his face said.

My fists clenched. I hated our silent conversations, but since neither of us could be civil to each other, silent was the only form of communication we had. And even silent we couldn't keep our emotions from unraveling.

"Ripper's going to take me for a ride tonight!" Anabeth said excitedly.

I glared at him. I just bet you are.

He glared back. What's wrong, baby? ZZ not givin' you the kinda ride you need?

Shut. Up.

He raised an eyebrow. Hittin' a nerve, huh?

Not. Anabeth, I begged him with my eyes. Please. Not. My. Friends.

Ripper's scar-slashed mouth twisted into a mocking smirk. Oh, so now there are rules? You can fuck my friends but I can't fuck yours? Don't exactly seem fair, baby.

Ripper kept his gaze on me while he slid his arm around Anabeth's shoulders and began tracing her collarbone with the tip of his finger.

"'Bout that ride, beautiful girl, where you wanna go?"

Anabeth, hearing the words "beautiful girl" in reference to her, beamed up at him.

Me, hearing the words "beautiful girl" come out of Ripper's mouth directed at anyone who wasn't me, had my insides roiling. Seeing this, Ripper looked triumphant.

What's wrong, Danny? You look upset. Was it somethin' I said?

I covered my mouth with my hand and tried to stay calm. Looking anywhere but at Ripper, I caught eyes with Kajika, a young Native American woman from a nearby Indian reservation who Cox and Kami had employed as their nanny.

She was beautiful, with long black hair and unforgettable, exaggerated features. Her eyes, nearly black and framed with thick, lush lashes, were all too knowing for my comfort.

Smiling kindly at me, she only made my already combative emotions that much worse. She could see right through me, everything I tried to hide. I hated being around her. She made me doubt every decision I'd made during the past three years. With just one damn look.

"'Scuse me," ZZ said, sidling up next to me and taking my hand in his. "I need my girl."

As Ripper stiffened, his arm falling away from Anabeth, I glimpsed the pain he hid beneath the anger.

Swallowing hard, I turned away from the group and let ZZ lead me out into the center of the lawn, where he pulled me into a bear hug.

"Don't hate me," he whispered. I glanced up at him, confused.

"What? Why would I hate you?"

He grinned, then dropped to his knees.

Correction. He dropped down on one knee. Heart pounding, not breathing, I stared down at ZZ, watching as he pulled a small black box out of his leathers. He looked up at me.

"You're the most beautiful woman I have ever seen," he said softly. "The sweetest and the kindest, too. You make me so fuckin' happy, baby, you make life so fuckin' good. So I'm askin' you if you'll marry me and let me spend the rest of my life tryin' to do the same for you."

He flipped the box open and revealed the biggest diamond ring I had ever seen.

"Oh … my … god," I whispered hoarsely, putting a shaking, sweating hand over my heart. I realized then that the yard had gone silent. Someone had shut the music off and all conversation had ceased.

I took a quick look around the yard. Everyone was grinning, smiling, and staring right at me.

This was bad. Very, very bad.

"Baby girl!" My head jerked at the sound of my father's voice.

"You say the fuckin' word and I will throw that asshole into next fuckin' week! Fact, whether you say yes or no, I'm still gonna beat the fuckin' shit outta him!"

Eva, who'd joined him, planted her palms in his stomach and playfully shoved at him. He captured her around her neck and pulled her up against him, all the while smiling at me.

ZZ must have already asked him. There was no way my father would have appreciated this being sprung on him. My father was the sort of man who had to mentally prepare himself for things like his daughter being proposed to.

Which meant ... my father was A-OK with me marrying ZZ.

In fact, looking around at all the happy faces, everyone was A-OK with me marrying ZZ.

More than okay. Elated, really.

Everyone except one.

I zeroed in on Ripper, whose sun-kissed skin had gone an interesting shade of green.

Our gazes locked.

And for a moment ... I thought I saw the man I loved.

Ripper stared at Danny. Stared at ZZ kneeling on the grass in front of her, asking her to marry him.

He was going to flip his shit.

These assholes all around him didn't realize it, but they were about to get sprayed with blood, bone, and brain when his head decided to explode, which was in about five motherfucking seconds.

Five ...

Four ...

Three …

Two …

One …

Fuck him.

Married.

ZZ was asking Danny to marry him.

Ah, fuck. What was happening to him? Everything inside of him suddenly felt all fucked-up and wrong. His heart started beating faster and his skin began to tingle irritably. The air around him grew thick, stuffy, making it hard to breathe. He felt lightheaded, his nose stung, and his stomach clenched painfully.

Before he began shredding his own body to pieces, just to make all these damn uncomfortable and unwanted feelings go away, he grabbed Anabeth and yanked her up against him. She responded immediately and curled seductively around his body.

Feeling like ten times an asshole, he kept his gaze on Danny as he groped Anabeth's ass.

Danny's beautiful blue eyes filled with pain and her gaze dropped back to ZZ.

He stopped breathing. She was going to say yes.

Say something, his brain screamed. STOP HER!

FUCKING STOP HER!

But he didn't.

He never did.

Because he was a useless pussy, who would never fucking deserve her.

So he just stood there like an asshole, manhandling her friend, and watching in horrified fascination as her lips parted and—

FUCK THIS SHIT.

Fuck the club and the code, and fuck brotherhood.

He would give it all up for her. For his woman. Because she sure as shit was his, and he'd go to hell and back ten times over before he lost her forever.

He shoved Anabeth aside, his right foot moved, and …

"DANNY!" he bellowed. "BABY!"